ASHISH CHAUHAN

STHITAPRAGYA

The Process of Maintaining Equilibrium

A memoir by **MAYOOR SHAH**

ASHISH CHAUHAN

STHITAPRAGYA

The Process of Maintaining Equilibrium

A memoir by **MAYOOR SHAH**

Published by
Mayoor Shah
Mumbai

First edition : **February 2021**

Cover Design : **Niraj Karvir**

Printed by : **Nine Square Prints (India) Pvt. Ltd.**
Royal Enclave, 113, 1st Floor,
Next to Sona Udyog Bhavan,
Parsi Panchayat Road,
Andheri (East), Mumbai – 400 069.
Tel. : 91-22 6628 5656
Mob. : 91-9820557212

Price : ₹ 500

Acknowledgments

My heartfelt thanks and gratitude to

Mr. Rahul Vyas, Mr. Gaurav Bangia and **Mr. Yash Shah,**

for their support throughout the process of writing this memoir.

Mayoor Shah

CONTENTS

AUTHORS NOTE

Ashish Chauhan is an enigma for people who have known him. He is one of the thought leaders and doers of modern Indian finance and society. He has been at the right place at the right time during the phase of liberalized India, post 1991.

His humble demeanour, easy conversational style, incisive comments, detailed understanding, complete control over situations and lack of personal desires suggests that he belongs to a different era. After a few minutes of interaction with him, one realizes that one has come in contact with a great soul - a wise old man in the guise of a young face - a modern Rishi. Despite leading a hectic social life, handling many important responsibilities, he is always unruffled and yet remains involved. He is connected to the core, but way above the basics of his existence.

I made a very short film on Ashish Chauhan on his 50th birthday because of Rahul Vyas, a friend and came in contact with Ashishbhai at that time. Although it was purely professional assignment, during our interactions his calm personality and complete lack of ego convinced me that I had come in touch with someone who is not only interesting but inspirational. That's what attracted me to the concept of writing a book on his journey so far.

When I broached the topic of writing a book, he was embarrassed. He kept on insisting that his life story is not interesting enough and people will not find the book useful at all. After a lot of convincing, he agreed. As we began to converse I thoroughly enjoyed the process, each session introduced me to his vast and varied vision with a touch of deep philosophy.

He also delayed and tried to resist the release if the book. After a lot of cajoling and follow up, I think, I have been able to write a meaningful story of his life. It is by no means a complete story. Neither is it his autobiography. It is something that I have figured, based on his memories narrated by him and people known to him. It is the painstaking work of over two years that has finally culminated in this book.

I hope, I have done some justice to his philosophy and his persona in this short book titled 'Stithpragya' - a Sanskrit word meaning – 'being equanimous under all circumstances' - the one who cannot be moved emotionally. The closest English word that comes to mind is 'Stoic', but in a very Indian way.

I hope readers will find this book useful in tracing the story of Ashish Chauhan and connect it to many important aspects of modern Indian finance, stock markets, derivatives, mutual funds, information technology, mobile and satellite telecom, retail, oil and gas, industry, education, corporate governance, sports, policy making, social progress, technological progress and many other areas in which he has played a major role since past three decades.

He is a poster child of India's progress and how life of every Indian citizen has changed over last 50+ years. He is unassuming, unattached, humble, confident and wise beyond words and years.

Of course he has got many more decades left to serve the country. In that context, this book should be taken as a comma, a prelude for greater things to come, rather than a full stop.

I am sure he will continue to chug along in his own measured, peaceful, wise and unattached ways as he has done all these years and keep making India proud.

MAYOOR SHAH

PREFACE

Ashish Chauhan's family hails from a small hamlet, near Ahmedabad, in Gujarat.

His father, a civil engineer and mother, a gold medallist in Economics, were both in Government service. A frugal and pious lifestyle at home had so greatly influenced little Ashish, that it was almost a foregone conclusion, among his family members, that he would embrace monkhood when he grew up! On the contrary, he was a 'happy go lucky' child, content with all that he had.

Education was of prime importance in his family, both his parents being well educated. But young Ashish was at ease with his studies, never under stress to outperform his peers. He was happiest outdoors! Affable by nature, he loved sports, especially cricket. His people connect was so good that he made his mark at organising events. He also had a huge appetite for the written word, a voracious reader of books on religion and philosophy in Gujarati. And as he grew up, this appetite increased as also the range of subjects, a habit that continues to be his favourite even today!

On such a carefree and simple substratum, his higher education and then his professional endeavours, built an edifice of remarkable achievements. He completed his graduation and post graduation from the most prestigious institutions in India, the 'Indian Institute of Technology', Bombay and the 'Indian Institute of Management', Calcutta, of course with some difficulties.

Having studied only in Gujarati during his entire schooling, up to 12th standard, English was his 'Achilles heel'. It took him time and lot of efforts to overcome this inhibition. Fortunately his deep involvement in extracurricular activities gave him some relief during those tough times. He honed his organisational capabilities by managing larger events and enjoyed developing interpersonal relationships with all strata of people. He enriched his life with solid friendships, a major support and influence in his life journey.

As soon as he secured his first job, it seemed fated that the toughest challenges were just waiting for him! Fearless by nature, each challenge not only gave him an adrenaline rush but also helped him develop many skills, in his quest to find solutions.

Ashish was working in core sector fields at a crucial time when India had started adopting 'technology' as the new mantra for progress. He started making great headways by adapting technology to address issues that were fettered with age old traditions and practices. This ushered in major changes and created many new benchmarks, speeding up the nation's progress. 'Speed' became his forte and 'Foresight', his fortitude.

Circumstances also favoured this spirited young man by handing him diverse opportunities on a platter and he converted each opportunity into an important milestone for the organisation he was working for. His work experience spans diverse sectors like Petrochemicals, Organised Retail, Oil & Gas, Cricket, Finance, Stocks and Trading etc.

Technology was the 'strategic' tool that he used in many brilliant ways. He encouraged his teams to drive existing or new technologies in different areas to help speed up operations and give faster results.

As he climbed the rungs of the corporate world, his achievements exemplified his philosophy, "if our thought process is attuned to overcome selfish interests and we purely seek a larger benefit, success cannot be far away." All his achievements showcase his dignified approach in gracefully accepting limitations and adapt to prevailing circumstances with zeal to overcome them.

A trail blazer in many areas, he spearheaded the success of a totally new concept - the 'NSE' and pioneered derivative trading in India, an achievement for which he has been acknowledged as the 'Father of Indian Derivative Market'. Later, as the CEO of the Bombay Stock Exchange he, along with his team, simultaneously worked on many fronts to transform the 145 yr old institution into one of the fastest and most admired Stock Exchanges in the world.

India lives in its people settled in remote villages and towns, the youth in mofussil areas are no less in their capabilities. His growth trajectory is an inspirational story of how India allows its youth to dream and also to achieve those dreams, provided they put in single minded efforts and work for their fellow beings.

As the book unfolds, chapter by chapter, we travel along with him on an interesting journey of discipline, hard work, a positive attitude, fearlessness, a balanced mind and above all, selfless service.

He inspires us with his attitude of being unattached to both success and failure, a must for every human being. He flows with the times, performs his duties without any self interest and sees the 'tomorrow' in all his endeavours.

'yaḥ sarvatrān-abhisnehas tat tat prāpya śubhāśubham |
nābhinandati na dveṣṭi tasya prajñā pratiṣṭhitā'

'He who has no attachment anywhere, who, when encountering the agreeable or the disagreeable feels neither attraction nor aversion, his wisdom is firmly established'

And so this book is aptly titled **'STHITAPRAGYA'**

STHITAPRAGYA

Chapter 1

Nascent Awakenings ..... *a blissful childhood.*

'It is better to live your own destiny imperfectly than to live an imitation of somebody else's life with perfection.'

Bhagwad Geeta

As I stepped into my chambers, a beautiful blue sky beckoned me towards the window. Here I was, on the 25th floor of the most prestigious building of Mumbai, P.J. Tower, the BSE building, India's premier Stock Exchange.

I glanced towards the sky, admiring the few stray white clouds dotting the blue expanse and then my eyes wandered down the street below. Among the hustle bustle of the people hurrying to their offices, I noticed an 8 to 10 year old young boy holding a cricket bat. Was he looking at me? His gaze was defined and his sparkling eyes shone bright, basking in the sunlight. Suddenly he lifted his hand and waved at me, with a cheerful and rapid motion - 'come down'. Was he telling me to come down?

He was, of course!

I smiled and waved back, indicating 'Wait, I am coming down'. My hurried steps into the corridor and towards the lift must have surprised my colleagues. It was so unlike a corporate official's stance, more childlike and joyful. In the lift, I could not help chiding myself "what am I doing? Am I hallucinating! What if he was not there?" But there was something palpable and intriguing about him which I just couldn't overlook!

Stepping out on the street, my nervous wandering glance could not conceal my apprehension. He was there! It was not an illusion! A few rapid strides in his direction brought me face to face with him. He stretched out his tiny palms and said "I am Ashish from Kochrab, Ahmedabad, remember me?"

From a narrow street of Mumbai, little Ashish transported me to Kochrab, Ahmedabad, my hometown in Gujarat. This was the village (now a part of Ahmedabad) where Mahatma Gandhi had set up his first ashram before shifting to Sabarmati.

I was born as the second child of Manilalbhai and Muktaben Chauhan at the V. S. Hospital in Madalpur, Ahmedabad. My sister Beena was two years older than me, she being the first born. After me came my brother Sunil, when I was 11, which made us a family of five. But we were not a nuclear family. Being a part of a joint family there were at least 8 to 10 people of all ages living with us. Since my birth we had shifted houses almost 3 to 4 times, finally settling at

Vasna, then on the outskirts of Ahmedabad, now a part of the mega city.

Our family hailed from a tiny village called Bavla, at that time located on the far outskirts of Ahmedabad. My father, being a civil engineer handling irrigation projects, was transferred from site to site and so he was constantly on the move. Because our house used to be closer to the city, there was a continuous flow of relatives coming to stay with us, some for studies and some for work.

Our living standards were very simple. Luxuries of any kind were never aspired. A single small room accommodated all eight to ten of us living happily. 'Live life as it comes' was the principle of my parents and elders, following the teachings of the religious faith we all followed.

Ours was a double income household, a rarity during those times, because both my parents were working. But even their combined income didn't fetch us any comforts, because they were taking care of the extended family and spending on their education too! Since there were hardly any savings, the thought of constructing our own house was a dream. In those times, as per our economic strata, building a house was considered a lifetime achievement, the highest aim for the lower middle class community.

Young Ashish was walking with me down the streets of Kochrab towards my home, holding my hand. Once we reached, he opened the door. I saw my mother, sitting near the 'sigdi (coals burned in a clay pot), making ' rotis'(round flatbread made from wholemeal flour). As usual she was hurrying up with her household chores because she had to rush to her office. She worked as an Inspector at the Sales Tax Office. My grandmother, Galalben, was sitting in one corner reciting her prayers. Having a sweet grandmother at home was a blessing for us.

My father, usually posted at various construction sites, was hardly at home. It was my mother, who had to manage everything.

This beautiful sight brought a flood of sweet memories of my early childhood!

The tenacity of my mother was admirable. She worked ceaselessly, taking care of a very large family, which included my cousins. She went about doing her chores cheerfully, from cooking food to cleaning vessels to washing clothes, apart from attending to her office duties. The routine at home was set, a meal served at 8 am every morning before mother left for work and dinner at 6.30 in the evening, with nothing cooked during the day.

My mother hailed from a comparatively affluent family, who had their origins in Karachi, now in Pakistan. However they had shifted to Khetwadi, Mumbai, before her birth. Her father ran a flourishing embroidery business in Mumbai initially and later shifted to Ahmedabad. His untimely demise, when she was quite young, led to closure of his business. She had three brothers studying in various streams; one became a doctor, another professor and the third, a banker. None of them was interested in running their embroidery business.

Her devotion was unparalleled. Her stoic acceptance of situations and circumstances was very graceful. She exemplified selfless service, bereft of any desire for personal benefits.

When I was around ten years old, my mother developed a thyroid dysfunction and started gaining a lot of weight resulting in very high blood pressure, but she continued working. Since there was an acute shortage of medicines in those days, I had to go from shop to shop to buy medicines for her. Due to her high blood pressure she had to be on a salt less diet. So food cooked at home went through three stages. The first stage was salt less and without onion and garlic, because she didn't eat garlic and onion. At the second stage salt was added, since some of us didn't eat garlic and onion and then at the third stage onion and garlic was added for the rest of the family members.

My father, a very strict disciplinarian would walk almost 5 to 6 kilometres every day, a discipline that he has maintained even today at the age of 80. He had a much regimented lifestyle. Whenever he was home, which was infrequent, he would make us children work hard too, either cleaning or constructing or moving furniture etc. I, not being strong physically, would try and always shirk from doing any strenuous physical activity.

Whenever my father was at home he always recited the 'Geeta dhwani' in Gujarati, a melodious poetry summarising the teachings of the Bhagwad Geeta and as he sung, we would sing along. This was followed by a daily puja ritual which was very invigorating. Till date the first salary of each child in the family goes to Dakorji temple, as a family tradition.

When I was 11 years old Pramukhswamiji , the head of the 'Swaminarayan' sect, himself baptized me in front of thousands of other children and I gave up eating onion and garlic from that day.

Both my parents were honest to the core. Being in government service, they never took undue advantage of their position or power. I distinctly remember my father's anger at being offered a pen as a gift; he threw that pen at the person. Another unique phenomenon was that he never bought any vehicle. We had to commute on foot or on bicycles. Till date he does not own a vehicle and prefers public transport!

Galalben, my grandmother, used to delight us with her narration of vivid memories of early 1900's, just after her marriage. A cheerful lady, she was very charitable and full of love for her grand children which even included children of our neighbourhood. Even at the ripe age of 90 she managed to remain active, going about doing her own chores.

For her, certain rituals were a must. The first 'roti' cooked every day was fed to a cow. She fasted on all auspicious days and would walk to the temple every morning. Observing her routine, we have subconsciously imbibed a set of values that we cherish till date.

I had a very interesting relationship with my grandmother. She was always eager to know what was happening in the world and I, or one of us children, had to read her the newspaper every day. To overcome her dependency on us she did display a tremendous eagerness to read and write and so we began teaching her the alphabets. We tried and tried but to no avail. She neither managed to read nor write! When I was 14, a cow hit her when she was on her way to the temple and since then she became bedridden till she breathed her last. Her selfless love, affection and childlike curiosity had filled our childhood with laughter and endearment.

Among some of my regular chores during childhood, one was to fetch 'ration'. In those days basic food grains like rice and wheat etc. were given at subsidised rates by the government based on the number of family members.

I remember standing in long queues for fetching our ration at the shop and it was often that by the time it was my turn, the shop would close! And so I was back in the queue once again the next day.

One of my fixed monthly duties was to travel to Relief road in Ahmedabad, to deposit my mother's savings in her recurring bank account there. This visit served two purposes; depositing monies and buying vegetables. I was given two large bags, which I hung on either side of the handle of my bicycle, to fetch vegetables from distant wholesale markets, at cheaper rates, so that we could economise on our food expenses.

Vacation time meant us going to stay at a nearby ancestral village. In that village there were a lot of cotton farms all around. The owners of cotton ginning mills in the city used to give the cotton produce, in measured quantities, to the housewives in the village, so that they would shell them and earn some money as well as use the shells for fuel at home. It was good income for them and beneficial to the mill owners too, as they didn't have to employ labour. These housewives would save this money to buy gold. My aunts used to do the shelling and we children were sent off to the ginning mills, carrying the shelled cotton!

In those times riots were commonplace in Ahmedabad, that too at frequent intervals, which got a communal flavour over a period of time. As children we used to see deaths at close quarters so often that we instinctively learnt the art of self survival and that in turn inculcated fearlessness.

Fearlessness became an integral part of my being since early childhood. This spirit helped me a lot when I started facing professional challenges later on.

The scenario at that time was perhaps ignited more because of rising unemployment, as large textile mills were closing down due to heavy taxation. With the advent of power looms, the focus on textiles shifted to the city of Surat. So the unemployed youth had a lot of free time and easily fell prey to these antisocial activities.

Gujarat used to face acute water shortage, due to lack of rainfall and poor water supply management in the city, so every drop of water was sparingly used. The climatic conditions here had made the city dry and there used to be a consistent problem of draught, periodically.

All these vivid memories of an innocent and carefree childhood, with its vagaries flashed in front of my eyes like a cinema. I was lost in the streets and fields around my house, the fragrance of mother earth surrounding me.

Little Ashish, standing by a bicycle, poked at me and said "do you remember how many times you have been taken to the bone setter?"

I usually walked to my school, which was about 3 to 4 kilometres from home. Occasionally, I was taken on a bicycle by some elder who was staying with us. Sitting behind on the bicycle, my foot used to often get entangled in the spokes of the wheels and I had to be immediately taken to a bone setter. This type of comic mishap must have happened at least 7 to 8 times in 5 years! After the pain I endured with the bone setter's sudden jerk, the best way to pacify me was with an icc cream from a lone 'Vadilal' ice cream shop nearby. Vadilal is now a big chain of ice cream shops all over India.

I remembered another unusual incident. I was just 5 yrs old when we had all gone to Gondal, a small town, for my maternal uncle's wedding. There I wandered off alone, to buy an 'ice gola' (ice sphere laden with rose syrup), and then I couldn't find my way back! Feeling lost, I started crying. People around me asked me where my home was but I couldn't answer. Then someone put me on a bicycle and took me around, so I could identify my home, but even that didn't help. Suddenly someone got a bright idea and started enquiring if any 'baraat' (wedding procession) had arrived from another town? That clue helped and I was safely handed over to my parents.

Little Ashishkumar and I were watching children playing. He nudged me again, "at such an early age you became so sensitive to issues of class and wealth divide, didn't you?

In my school, some school mates belonged to affluent families from business backgrounds while some were from poor families. Since most of the families living in my neighbourhood were from economically weak strata of society, we didn't envy the affluent children.

I studied in a Gujarati medium school. The State of Gujarat had become independent of Maharashtra in 1960, and Gujarati, as a language, was promoted with a sense of pride, hence English was considered a secondary language.

Since my school was at a distance, I had two groups of friends, one group consisted of my school friends and the other group was friends that I made near my home. These two sets of friends were poles apart in their demeanour.

Near my home there were hutments occupied by 'Rabaris' (cowherds) and it was their children with whom I played, along with other children. Due to abject poverty these Rabaris faced extreme hardships. Observing their struggles, I used to consider myself lucky to have a family which could feed me and educate me.

Among my school friends I was perceived as 'aggressive', because they were very mild and well mannered. In contrast, among my home friends I was perceived as meek, because the Rabaris and other children near my house were very aggressive in nature.

The class divide and the social structure that existed was something that bothered me, and it had left a deep impression on me then, which made me sensitive to this issue.

We used to frequently visit our extended family members living in our village, about 30 kilometres away. Be it an occasion or not, a visit to meet our cousins was a must.

At that tender age I could closely observe that the villages, contrary to popular perception, were cesspools of injustice and discrimination between the rich and the poor. The poor were not given a chance to uplift themselves. Even the smartest among them would be exploited. Poor families had to suffer severe indignities every day, their women and children being the most vulnerable. Providing justice to them was out of question, as any ruling, which was much delayed, was always in favour of the dominant group, which was the slightly affluent class.

With such discrimination and indifference, the poor couldn't come out of their poverty, ever! Even a marginal increase in their living standards would be watched keenly by the others who would try to take it away by brute force or chicanery.

Here children, at the age of two or three, either learnt to dominate, if they were affluent or to act subservient, if they were poor. By the time they grew up, everything was set for them; they were cast in the mould, set as per social norms.

Due to rampant corruption there was abundance in some families, who lived a life without conscience. In deep contrast there were those living in abject poverty, who made all efforts to live gracefully, following virtuous values of humanity.

A deep rooted empathy for those who had no opportunity to grow or be socially accepted kept fanning my mind. This double faced society and its impact on the people somehow affected me and I resolved that in whatever capacity I could, I would try and always help the poor, as they had every right to live a life of dignity.

This day to day exposure to the social injustice, on so many occasions, made me wonder how the society could easily drive any person to resort to criminal acts. Even I could have succumbed to the morass or criminality, which would have been very difficult to come out of. What saved me was my upbringing that had me grounded. It's such bliss to be content, and not crave for what is not yours!

In moments of solitude a question kept haunting me 'Why can't our country free its poor children from the shackles of shortages and exploitation? How can we eradicate this evil from our society, created by the 'haves' and free our nation from a class divide.

This awareness was beneficial throughout my growing years, and actually became an asset in making me emphatic towards people from all strata of society.

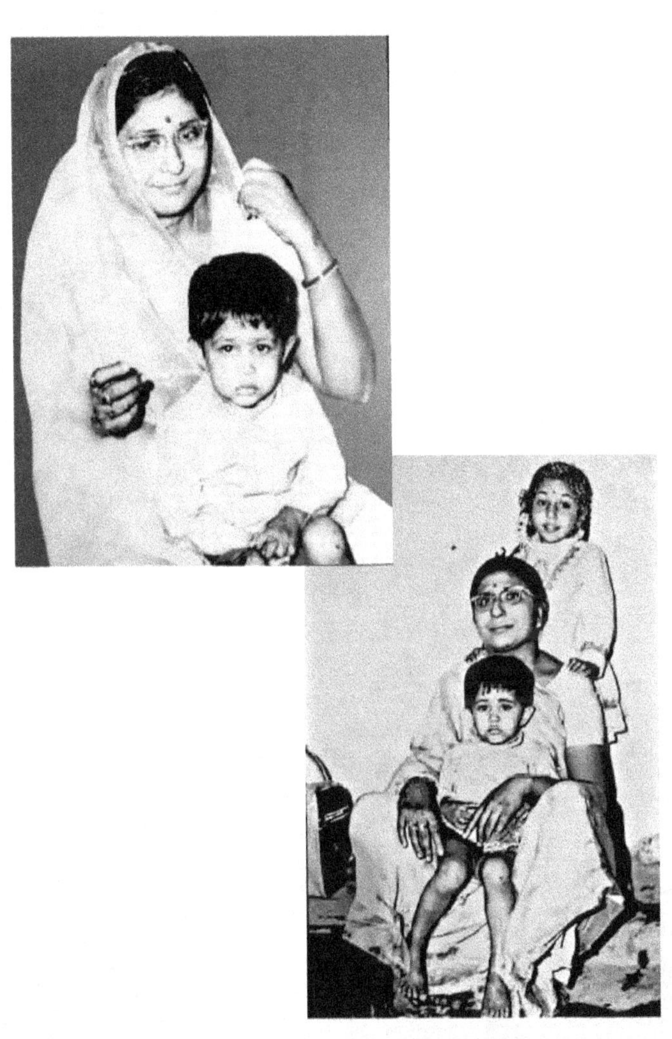

STHITAPRAGYA

Chapter 2

The Cosy Cocoon ....*carefree school life.*

"Give freely. Be self-controlled, sincere, truthful, loving, and full of desire to serve. Realize the truth of the scriptures learn to be detached and to take joy in renunciation."

Bhagwad Geeta

Deeply engrossed in a serious thought, I was pulled out from my reverie. Little Ashish was waving a magazine he had picked up from a shelf in my house. His genuine smile made me remember my fondest passion.

Reading was an obsession for me. In a week I would perhaps read more than 500 pages, apart from all the newspapers and my study material!

We had over 10 magazines delivered regularly at home, 'Ramakadu', 'Champak', 'Chandamama', 'Rang Tarang', 'Jan

Kalyan', 'Akhand Anand', 'Chitralekha' 'Abhiyan' and others. It was only me and my mother who would read them.

I even read translated books by some Russian authors like Tolstoy, Dostoevsky, Karl Marx and Lenin etc, because these were distributed free of cost. Then there were books by well known Gujarati authors like Kanhaiyalal Munshi, Umashankar Joshi, Vinod Bhatt and Joseph Macwan, all of whom I loved.

Philosophy and religion too were my favourite subjects. I used to read the translated versions of Hindu scriptures like the Vedas, Upanishads and books on Buddhism and Jainism. My inquisitive mind was keen to seek answers to my questions about our existence. The eight fold path of Buddhism really inspired me, leaving a deep imprint on my mind at that age. I will further elaborate on my views on religion and philosophy in a dedicated chapter.

Ashish laughed and said 'reading was of such great interest, you could have been a scholar, but did you ever take the word 'study' seriously?"

It was so true. For me studies were a very casual affair, easy and effortless. I was never under stress to get a good rank. Everyone expected me to be among State toppers in the 10th and 12th standards, while I didn't even remotely consider working towards that goal. Both these crucial years, I didn't even come in the top ten rankings. I was perhaps one among the 100 or 200!

Studies and academics were not as compelling as my extracurricular activities, a contradiction of sorts. Little did I know that, later, academics were to become the core driving force in my life.

Ashish jutted in, swinging his bat, "You were such an outdoor person!"

I was happiest playing cricket, the field was my arena of joy. Unfortunately buying a good cricket bat was out of question as we couldn't afford it and coupled with this drawback was my poor eyesight, which put an end to my cricketing aspirations as a full time career.

Playing cricket with spectacles was discouraged because of an incident in my family. My first cousin had spectacles and used to play cricket. Once the ball hit his eyes so badly that it affected his vision permanently. His father, my maternal uncle, was an eye surgeon and had immediately conducted a surgery, but he continued to have problems with his vision.

Playing apart, watching cricket matches was also a craze for me and my friends. Since we didn't have Television at home, we used to identify homes with antennas, which were a little further away from our neighbourhood. We would then queue up in front of those houses as early as 7 am. And they were kind enough to allow us to watch television during days of the match, plus feed us too! Such genuine hospitality by them, for us children from distant locality, was such a warming gesture.

This experience encouraged my family to make TV accessible to as many cricket lovers as possible. When my family bought a T V in 1983, we would keep it outside during matches, facing the road so that others could watch it sitting in our compound.

1978 onwards the India Pakistan series were telecast live on an experimental basis and Ahmedabad was one of the chosen cities. I was fortunate to have seen many of them.

Till date cricket remains a passion for me. Even during the professional phase of my life I would play a lot of cricket on weekends. You will be amazed to know that cricket had some organic connection later in life.

Chess was another sport I indulged in and surprisingly excelled in too. Around the age of 8 or 9, I learnt to play chess by accident. Very soon I started defeating everyone in my age group and practically everyone in my area. I was then regularly called by a National chess 'B Group' Championship player, so that he could practice his moves and he too got defeated in some of our games!

His brother was a boxer. Out of curiosity for that sport, I started learning boxing from him. But my constitution was not strong enough to withstand hits and I ended up hurting myself badly within a few sessions, so my boxing experience ended abruptly.

Ashish laughed "You? A boxer!

Till the age of 14, I was really short and my friends were growing taller! Even my sister was way taller compared to me. To make me gain height I was subjected to a lot of experiments, the funniest one being making me drink camel milk for months together. My height started to increase only when I was around 15 and by 17, I became a decent 5 feet 7 inches tall, which we consider normal in India.

A nudge again from the little boy, "and your daredevil attempts during Diwali, remember them?"

Festivals were occasions I enjoyed a lot, be it Garba and Raas during Navratri, or celebrations like Holi, Diwali and Uttarayan (Kite festival). But I was given strict instructions to be home before 9 pm. Only during Navratri, I was allowed to stay out late in the night.

With limited pocket money, during Diwali we would buy rockets at the lowest cost. These rockets, costing 10 paisa per piece, wouldn't fly off unless you actually threw each by hand after lighting them. We would first light a rocket in our hands and then casually throw it up in the air, some 100 or 200 of them in an hour. There was never a fear of explosion or burns!

Kite flying was another addiction. A month after Diwali all of us would start flying kites. It was a daily routine in the morning and evening on the days when we had school. And on holidays it was for the entire day if we were not playing cricket. It was such a matter of pride to show off how many kites we managed to snip or catch.

Most of our vacations would usually be spent at home or in our village, which was just an hour's journey from home. Rarely did we go far. If we did, it was for a couple of days on a minor travel on LTA of my parents, or we would go to my maternal uncle's place in Bhachau, Kutch, where he was in charge of an eye hospital.

Academics were an important lifeline for my extended family too!

I had observed that everyone's career was a straight and defined path and education was the only way to success in life. Almost all my family members were in salaried jobs, barring a few, who did attempt business. But when they failed, they too resorted to taking up jobs.

On completion of higher studies the first choice was to seek a government job, which we believed was most stable. Therefore, if a child in the family was good in studies he would become an officer and if he was weak in studies, he would become either a clerk or do some administrative job in a Bank or a private sector organization.

My father had 2 brothers and 2 sisters. My elder uncle used to run a small shop in the village but the earnings were not sufficient for him to run the household. He was the closest relative I knew, who did business. He expired when I was young. On his death, one of his sons, my first cousin took over the shop.

One of our neighbours had a shop which sold saris. He was a retail and wholesale distributor of variety of saris. However, I couldn't gain any business knowledge because of complete discouragement from home.

Other neighbours were either doing jobs or were small time artisans. Yes, one of my cousins was enterprising and he managed to evolve himself into being a businessman, much later.

With no exposure to business none of us children had any inkling of trade or manufacturing. "We can't do business as our risk taking ability is zero, and we don't have the capital" was the narrative at home.

In such a scenario I was lucky to have been exposed to a business application in a small way. Some of my friends showed a spark of entrepreneurship at a very young age. They started earning when the VCR was introduced in the market. The older boys began organizing screening of films on some terrace, selling tickets at ₹ 1 each. Getting an audience was not difficult as there were many who were ready to pay to watch the latest movies. We were too young to handle money, so the older lot would make us to do menial work, like getting electrical connections on the terrace and make seating arrangements etc. Our reward was watching the movies for free! Some of my childhood friends later set up cable TV operations in our area, as their business.

Little Ashish was wandering a little away. I took a few fast paced steps to catch up with him. He smiled and said, "This is where you grew up and look where you have settled now!"

My first visit to Mumbai, called Bombay at that time, was when I was around 7. My father's younger brother, a gold medallist in Geography, was appointed as a Professor in Mumbai. All of us went to Mumbai to see him during one of our vacations. He couldn't host us all, as he himself shared an apartment with some people. So we stayed with some other relatives for a couple of days. That was the time we commuted by trains in Mumbai. I never imagined that this hustling bustling city was to become my home later!

Experiencing Mumbai was an eye opener for me. I was in awe of this fast moving city where even trains didn't stop for more than a few seconds at any station. Everyone looked busy. The only thing I didn't like about Mumbai was that it looked dirty as compared to Ahmedabad. Sadly, the difference in cleanliness still exists between two cities!

Little Ashish had smartly brought me back to the present and disappeared!

Someone tapped me on my shoulder, "Ashish Sir, what are you doing on the road', need some help?" It was one of my colleagues. Embarrassed, I mumbled something and started to stroll back towards the office building, in a dream like state.

As I walked back to my chambers, I reminisced my childhood. It was such a 'happy go lucky' phase, I neither had needs of material things nor any direction.

There was no thought about the future, and there was nothing that I wanted from my parents. It was wonderful to be devoid of any expectations and needs that make our life complicated. Whatever was available was enough!

One predominant factor, a great gift of my childhood, was the influence of my grandmother, mother and sister. Their positivity, selfless service and acceptance of circumstances moulded my entire outlook towards life.

I was brought up as a normal child with the right values. But my parents were constantly worried because of my company of friends. And I kept my teachers constantly worried because I was too causal with my studies.

In hindsight I must say, things I didn't bother about in early childhood, did come back to haunt me later in my youth.

During my 12th Standard, a coaching class gave me free coaching, because they were sure I would be amongst the toppers in the Board exams or at least obtain highest marks in a few subjects. Neither of what they desired happened! But I was happy with the marks I obtained, although they were below expectations for all who knew me. They were still good enough for me to secure admission in any stream in a college of my choice.

After gallivanting happily through a carefree childhood, having given no importance to academics, my transition to higher studies was unbelievably smooth. I was now at that turning point of my life, which I never imagined would charter a unique path here on.

STHITAPRAGYA

Chapter 3

Chrysalis *......unfolding of wings*
Indian Institute of Technology, Bombay (1984 – 1988)

'You have control over doing your respective duty, but no control or claim over the result. Fear of failure, from being emotionally attached to the fruit of work, is the greatest impediment to success, because it robs efficiency by constantly disturbing the equanimity of mind.'

Bhagwad Geeta

My family, my home, my city and its culture was a comforting cocoon. But there was a much bigger world out there, and to see that I had no option but to fly!

Around Oct 1984, before my 12th standard exams, Utkanth Bhandari, my school friend, told me that he was applying for the Indian Institute of Technology, Joint Entrance Exams (JEE), for engineering stream and asked me if I would be interested. If so, he would fill in my form too.

I was completely unaware of IIT and its standing .The vernacular newspapers never had any information or articles on IIT. On the spur of the moment I casually said 'yes!' I had actually given no serious thought to further studies, in spite of the fact that my family believed that this was the only way to secure a job! Utkanth applied and we were called for entrance exams.

My father, being an engineer, was aware of IIT. Our JEE for IIT were to be held at IIT campus in Mumbai, due to ongoing riots in Gujarat.

So Utkanth and I set out for Mumbai to take the entrance exams. This was my first visit to Bombay without my family members. We stayed at Kalyan at my friend's uncle's place and roamed all over the city by train. We also stayed at IIT Bombay campus for a couple of days, during exams. The seniors at IIT, noticing us as dumb youngsters, one among them began ragging us. I was ragged even before entering IIT as a student! Ironically, the same senior who ragged me then, is now one of my best friends.

I got through the entrance tests and obtained admission at IIT, Bombay, subject to clearing the 12th standard exam.

In June 1985 IIT commenced its curriculum for the first semester. I couldn't join because my 12th standard exams were postponed further.

In August, on the very first day of my exam, I got up with high fever, but I had the resilience to write my papers, so I went ahead and took the exam. I believe that the least we can do is to attempt. If we don't even try, failure is assured. The essence lies in attempting with all sincerity.

I joined IIT immediately after my 12th standard exams on the 13th of Sept, 1985. Almost half the courses in the first term at IIT were over by then!

I was allotted a room in the hostel called H6, where my predecessor had committed suicide, due to sheer pressure of studies. This had such a demoralising impact on me and it also set many a tongue wagging among batch mates, that Ashish will either run away or commit suicide!

Since childhood I had the habit of sleeping on a hard bed without any mattress on the floor or even on a wooden plank. I continued with this habit even in my hostel. Most of my friends couldn't manage to sleep on the floor even for a couple of hours.

Uprooted suddenly, I used to feel homesick and kept rushing to Ahmedabad almost every weekend. These frequent trips kept me sleepy headed in class. Also the climatic change and humidity of Mumbai began to take a toll on my health. I suffered from cold and cough, fever and uneasiness. Away from the familiar environs, I was trying to find roots in a new soil.

I had missed a lot of studies and the weekly exams at IIT, and had to cover six subjects, plus English. Since I could not cope up with so much pressure, I was compelled to drop two subjects.

At IIT, we also had to complete a sports activity. Without much thought, I chose mountaineering. It was a seven day excursion with walks uphill, mountaineering was the only sports subject I could hope to complete in the first term, due to my delayed joining. I had packed a regular bag, which I never realised would become so difficult for me to carry. Mountaineering was not meant for me. Fortunately my leaders, Ajay and Sadhana Shah volunteered to carry my bag, and in order to give me company, the entire team had to slow down. It was only on the third day that I got slightly acclimatised to the strain and somehow managed to complete this activity.

The biggest hurdle I faced at IIT was of language. Though there were quite a few students from vernacular medium schools, they had been taught in English in their 11th and 12th standards. For me it had been Gujarati throughout.

English perplexed me. It used to take me 3 to 4 hours to understand one page! I had to keep referring to my dictionary for almost every word. The formulas were fine, as they were in English and were taught in English even back home.

Lectures were difficult to comprehend. During viva's I remained tongue tied, I knew the answer, but speaking the language and its grammar, that too with my vernacular accent, was a major limitation. I used to feel ashamed because even peons there spoke in English. I immediately took up English speaking classes, with emphasis on pronunciations, to overcome my vernacular intonation.

The academic scuffle, however tough, somehow got me just below average marks in all my exams, something I was satisfied with. Thank god, there was no fierce ambition driving me to become a scholar of sorts.

At IIT, there developed a strange support system for me. One of my seniors Hemanshu Bhatt was like a paternal figure for me. He knew if I wasn't handled with care, I would run away, so he was always protecting me and guiding me. He even made me shift my room to his hostel wing, so that he could look after me.

Gajanan Gandhe and Makrand Agashe were my room partners in the first few years. C S Devashish took good care of me. All of them were very supportive teaching me English, guiding me on what books to read etc. We remain very emotionally bound till date, even though most have gone abroad. We just belong to each other.

I made a huge friend circle, my hostel mates, batch mates, and also friends from outside campus. I could blend easily with different sets of people.

At the end of the first year, I went back home. My father opined that I should at least try the local colleges and decide whether I need to go back to IIT, Bombay or pursue my second year in Ahmedabad.

Heeding to his suggestion, I attended the V S Medical College for a day. I found many of my school friends studying there, and though it was one of the best medical colleges, the stream didn't attract me.

I then went to L D Engineering College, tried it out for a few days, but unfortunately I ended up playing with friends, than attending classes.

Both the Medical and Engineering colleges were running late in their semesters due to delayed exams in Gujarat.

Somehow my instinct told me to continue at IIT, Bombay. I did not want to sacrifice one semester and lag behind, might as well go back and complete the term of 4 years.

In my second year at IIT, I opted for Mechanical Engineering.

My adrenaline at IIT Bombay was the vast scope of extracurricular activities that the Institute offered. In fact active participation in these also helped me shift focus from the travails I experienced in academics.

We had many cultural festivals at the Institute and to become a part of the organising team was both challenging and joyful, an activity I enjoyed since my school days. Our annual grand cultural event, 'Mood Indigo', had us hosting top notch musicians, rock bands, singers, dignitaries etc. Meeting them, dealing with them and managing logistics was fun. This learning experience was going to be immensely helpful much later in my career.

I was at ease in working with everyone, from the lowest to the highest authority. Being fair and transparent gave me the advantage of creating and concluding any event smoothly.

Then we had the 'Sports' and 'Technology' festivals, both my favourite.Within no time I earned a reputation as a 'go getter'. All my friends believed that I could manage gatherings well and soon I became the most trusted one to make any event successful in the campus.

It was here that I pioneered the International Society for Krishna Conscious-ness (ISKCON) weekly event. I invited their representatives to come and give discourses on the 'Bhagwad Geeta' and Krishna Consciousness, at the hostel. They always came with very good food, an incentive for many students to attend the event. My idea was to create more awareness on philosophy through these discourses, but it influenced some juniors so much that they opted to become monks! Such was the impact of this initiative.

At my hostel, I conducted a summer mess for the students who used to stay back during vacations and also for those who would come to do summer training or summer study. This concept worked well and soon it became a successful business venture. What seemed like a distant horizon and unknown territory to me in my childhood, at IIT an idea became a business opportunity which benefitted the hostel monetarily. Needless to say I had no interest in any personal profit.

But the distraction of too many extracurricular activities had its flip side; I developed a habit of staying up all night, and sleeping during the day. Lectures were missed and the company I kept induced me into drinking alcohol, eating non vegetarian food, smoking etc.

Perhaps it was to do with age of 18, being exposed to so many opportunities, a city life and so many outlets that a reckless attitude was setting in.

At some point of time, my mother came to know that her friend, Dr. Mrs Parikh, was a faculty member at the IIT, Bombay.

Professor Dr. Mrs Parikh had a son, Bhushan and daughter Meena. Meena was studying at the NID, Ahmedabad. Bhushan was doing Mechanical Engineering at REC, Surat. Mrs Parikh grew very fond of me and I got a mother figure in Bombay. Although they are not my relatives, they took care of me as their own kin and till date we introduce ourselves as cousins.

Mumbai is famous for its typical 'chawl' system of houses, usually either a single or just 2 rooms, with a long common balcony and common toilets. One of my aunts lived in a chawl, which soon became my favourite place to go to, for food and company, and it became a home away from home.

By the time I was in my 3rd year at IIT, I and Sharda Ranjan Pendharkar, a fellow student of Mechanical Engineering and my hostel mate, became inseparable. In one of the semesters, Sharda put in his nomination for the post of General Secretary at the Institute. He was already the General Secretary at the hostel. Someone from our friend circle informed his father, who got angry and refused to grant him permission to contest for that election, as he was already weak in his studies.

We quietly put in my name and I got elected without any opposition, as there was no other contestant. Now my father got angry, as I too was not performing well academically. I was called in by the authorities and had to put in my resignation.

This move created a big misunderstanding with one of my close friends Ramesh. He felt that we had done this deliberately to harm his chances at another post in the same election. Many of my juniors were also convinced about this. On our part, it was actually an act done without much logic and with no malice. After many years the enmity is now over, but this incident taught me a big lesson.

The years at IIT were the toughest part of my life. I was facing many hurdles mentally and physically. However, these tough times instilled a confidence in me that I could handle any situation. A selfless attitude used to drive me sub consciously which made it enjoyable. I never looked at the gain or loss, and had no attachment to material aspects or ego satisfaction.

During those years, I learnt about interpersonal behaviour patterns from friends of different calibre. Some of them were extremely disparaging and some were extremely helpful. The most wonderful moments of my life, some very enduring friendships and precious memories are the treasure of the four years at IIT, Bombay.

In my final year we had to do a large and significant, yearlong engineering project, like a thesis, to get our B Tech degree. I selected 'Gasifier and Automobile Engineering' as my topic, an opportune project destined to teach me the basics that would be invaluable for me later on.

Thanks to Prof. Mrs. Parikh and her laboratory, I got exclusive access to computers. The lab had several stand alone computers in those days. Even large companies didn't have them as they were exorbitant in price. As a part of the project, I had to collect 'real time' data on the computers, to measure the temperature, pressure etc. in order to optimise gasifier designs. We were also doing research on alternative fuels. This project became my tryst with technology.

Using the standalone computers was my first exposure to 'end to end' technology at work. There were no tutors to teach us operations, so we had to read the computer manuals and collate the data to see the results, an exercise that became the best learning experience! The confidence that our inputs will make a computer work by itself, made me very positive. Technology was now at my command and it was in my hands to get the best results.

I was introduced to a dream much larger than envisioned, and this helped me in make technology work on a massive scale much later. At this stage it was sheer magic for me.

In 1989, I completed graduation in the stipulated four years, though some of my friends had to spend a few more years, before they could graduate!

It was surely a Chrysalis! The complacent Ashish became a far more mature person, enriched with knowledge, thanks to an excellent faculty and friends. Added to this was a vast experience of organising and executing programmes and festivals on a large scale. And of course, the computers!

From an Institute that was supposed to teach higher level academics, I actually learnt more of life skills! But I must honestly confess that I do regret not studying more seriously. Had I focussed on studies, I could have added more to my academic skills!

STHITAPRAGYA

Chapter 4

Self Actualisation .... *realization of self potential*
    Indian Institute of Management, Calcutta (1989-1991)

"We must act in a selfless spirit, Krishna says, without ego-involvement and without getting entangled in whether things work out the way we want."

Bhagwad Geeta

Due to my initial difficulties at IIT, I believed that Engineering was not my forte; it was just by accident that I chose this stream, but that accident had its purpose. When I got my engineering exam results, it was shocking to note that my marks were higher than many other engineering students! This gave me an incentive to seek admission at the Indian Institute of Management, the most prestigious set of Management Institutes in India, and I got admission at IIM after passing the Common Competitive Test (CAT).

Soon I was at the Indian Institute of Management (IIM), Calcutta. The subjects I chose were Finance and Economics. My father was very surprised that I did not get admission at IIM Ahmedabd, but far away in Calcutta! It was natural for him to feel so, but he did not discourage me, and in fact supported me financially too.

Fate drew me to Calcutta for a reason. Since childhood I had read a lot about communism and leftist ideology. To experience it firsthand, Calcutta was the ideal city. It was a lazy city and people were least money minded, both these qualities were present in me too! Calcutta or Kolkatta as we now know it, of the 80's, was a city I immediately fell in love with. It still feels like my second home!

I remember a funny incident. Having been allotted a room in the IIM hostel, the first thing I did was remove the mattress on the bed, and keep it down. I would sleep on the wooden plank, and made the mattress a lounging seat for others! My new friends at IIM, Calcutta were highly amused to see this.

Another thing I noticed was that the bonhomie among students at IIM, Calcutta was in stark contrast to that of IIT. Here students came with a defined purpose, that of getting the best job in the best organisation! Most of them nurtured a great sense of insecurity within them. I found this to be a strange mindset, and soon became a bemused spectator to all this. For me, there was absolutely no fear or insecurity. I would get what I deserved was all I believed. I would not even give a second thought of being competitive with my friends.

All the students would get very upset when we used to get low marks in our tests, and I, having been used to low marks many times during my IIT days, used to wonder what all the fuss was about!

At IIM, attending lectures was not compulsory. In retrospect, I feel it was a great boon, as we learnt much more by being free from that compulsion.

I was back to my routine of being up during nights and sleeping during the day. Nights were for loitering around, or playing matches, either cricket or table tennis. In cricket, though I didn't have the demeanour of a fast bowler, I used to be good at taking wickets with a short run up and my batting was also not bad. However, most of the nights we played more of Table Tennis.

The IIM Calcutta campus was located at 'Joka', at that time far away from the main city. I and my friend, Sandip Seth, would roam around on his scooter. We would go for movies or visit interesting places. At that time Rabindra Setu was half built, so our favourite night spot was to go and sit there for hours, just to observe twinkling lights of the city. Sandip was from Mumbai. Unfortunately, he expired within a few years of our passing out, due to a cardiac arrest. I am still in touch with his brothers.

I used to get a lot of time to read and so those subjects that interested me drew me more and more towards self study. The self learnt, self researched content was a great help when I started writing articles for local and international publications.

One extremely useful skill I learnt here was typing. At IIT, we had to take service of typists, but at IIM, I did it myself and with continuous practice, managed to achieve a good speed. This skill was my saviour when I started working.

Quite a number of students were older to me. They were already in jobs and had come to complete their post graduation here. They came with their families for the entire term. I remember in my first year, I used to take care of my senior Vijay's daughter Aditi, as he was studying, and his wife was working in the city.

By the time I got into IIM, the fear of English had gone. Fortunately, my engineering background helped me understand statistics and related subjects more easily, which was usually a stumbling block for those who came from non engineering backgrounds. This knowledge in fact made me a little over confident. I found the curriculum here to be easier than that of IIT.

In my first year we had generic subjects. It was in the second year that we could choose specialised subjects of our interests. I used to be fascinated by Stock markets, not the typical study of the ups and downs, but the functioning and its nature of activities. Since I was bunking lectures, I got a lot of time to read books on stock markets. Observing this, my friends started believing that I was very good at investments!

At the end of the first year, I took up a summer job at 'ANZ Grindlays Bank', now bought over by Standard Chartered Bank. My portfolio was to handle sick companies referred to the Board of Industrial and Financial Reconstruction or BIFR. I began dealing with financial institutions and banks, and started gaining knowledge on the theory and practices of sick companies, a subject that was being researched at a global level. This stint was actually the prime motivator for me to seek a job in a financial institution after the second year.

The fine line between theory and practice now became clearer to me. We had to adapt the theory to prevalent conditions and changing parameters, and create the right solutions.

Developmental Economics was a subject that interested me most. It was different from modern economics. I had the great fortune to study under a renowned economist, Prof. Amit Bhaduri , who also developed a liking for me. Additionally, I chose to take a course on 'Econometrix', a subject no student usually opted to learn. On my request, Professor Mr. Reddy told me to gather 5 students, the minimum number required to offer this course.

With great sincerity I managed to convince four others, but I myself never attended a single lecture! During exams Professor Reddy chided me "Did you waste my time or did I waste your time?"

I completed the project work. Somehow, he was gracious and large hearted enough not to have failed me.

I believe that these were the years where learning happened at two levels. One was of course the 'academics', but the larger part was the learnings from peers, participating in lots of debates and discussions, managing new activities and exploring myself.

In hindsight, missing lecture sessions made me miss out on some vital interactions in the classroom; there could have been learning in that too! But I was on my own trip, doing what I wanted and honestly a trifle aimless too.

STHITAPRAGYA

Chapter 5

Preamble *...the tomorrow that came today!*
Industrial Development Bank of India (1991 -1993)

'Set thy heart upon thy work, but never on its reward. We behold what we are, and we are what we behold. Perform all work carefully, guided by compassion.'

Bhagwad Geeta

The intense reading I did in various topics related to Finance and Economics resulted in a growing desire to delve further. So at the end of the second year I had decided that I would apply for a job only in a financial institution and at that time there were just a handful!

My hometown being far off, almost a 60 hour journey, dissuaded me from travelling frequently. I would go home just once in a year. Now academics interested me.

The subjects were easier than those at IIT, my academic performance was far better, and the projects given to us were captivating. Gradually I began to develop new skill sets.

When IDBI, the Industrial Development Bank of India, called me for an interview, I actually had the audacity to go dressed informally to face eminent people. I was dressed in a casual T shirt, trousers and a pair of slippers. The interview was conducted by very senior officials including senior economists. As usual this interview began on a formal note, but as we interacted it turned out to be a long session of over one and a half hours, because they were impressed by my innate ability to converse on related topics with ease.

I got the job and my father was the happiest. For him a job in any public sector undertaking meant guaranteed lifetime security. He had always worked with the government, so he was satisfied at my having obtained a goal.

IDBI Bank, at that time, was the largest development bank in India. This placement was a sunrise opportunity at the very beginning of my career. I was handling project finances when India was witnessing all round growth, and we, at IDBI, were flooded with proposals of large set ups in various sectors. India was starting to liberate.

I was now passionately engaged in work and that too at an impatient speed. Speed was something that fascinated me like an eager child, who wanted results in a jiffy!

Those days, government organisations had so much manpower, that we were not allowed to type ourselves. Each officer was allotted a stenographer, plus we were not allowed to pick up files and give it to our superiors, that only the peons could carry to and fro, and clerks had to do the filing.

I was quite averse to these slow procedures, so I used to tell my steno to sit, while I typed the document myself and began to carry my files and papers to my bosses, convincing the peons that they should rest. I also did the filing myself. However, since the Unions were strong, I had to sign overtime forms for peons, clerks, stenos etc.

We had to work on detailed spreadsheets for project financing. As per norms, these involved lots and lots of calculations. A minor change under any head would affect the total working. As per routine, a spread sheet would first take weeks to create, as it was made using a manual calculator. If the authorities made a slight change, then it would again take weeks to re calculate. And the bosses seemed to be in no hurry, giving us ample of time!

It was a co incidence that IDBI had just acquired PCs and I could take full advantage of them to make calculations happen in seconds.

Now my papers reached the bosses in no time and whatever the change, I was back at their desk in a few minutes with the revised calculations .This sent a shock wave up in the hierarchy and I came into limelight as the 'fastest' officer. The computer was actually the real hero, but I was attributed for the speed, and that earned me a tag of a good 'IT professional!'

Information Technology wasn't even a remote choice for my career. However, IT came into my life to stay and fate had some challenging plans for me in this sector.

This was the year 1991, when we were working day and night on the innumerable possibilities of growth. I was agog with new energies and excitement and there was this inner urge to perform. I was working like an entrepreneur in a government organisation, doing everything myself, including cyclostyling sheets and delivering them to concerned people in the middle of the night, in taxis, before crucial meetings.

Speed of operations gave IDBI a new impetus and they decided to buy 1000 computers. This decision created a lot of anxiety about potential job losses among staff and officers alike, due to oncoming automation. IDBI went on a strike for months together. The employees would come to office and shout slogans instead of doing their work. The strike was called off only after promises were taken for no job loss whatsoever. This was my first hand experience of organised group behaviour.

The 'net' was cast by destiny, symbolically a preamble to a greater adventure!

STHITAPRAGYA

Chapter 6

The Labyrinth .....*an exalting phase*
National Stock Exchange (1993 - 1995)

'One is understood to be in full knowledge whose every endeavour is devoid of desire for sense gratification. He is said by sages to be a worker for whom the reactions of work have been burned up by the fire of perfect knowledge.'

Bhagwad Geeta

Perhaps being a Gujarati, finance and financial markets attracted me naturally. In those days all the correspondence and jargon used at the stock exchanges was in gujarati, which I could understand easily.

I was very fortunate to have taken interest in finance. I was literally in the midst of many a change that would create history in our country's progress.

Many believe that Finance is a complicated subject, but once you understand its principles, it's fascinating.

I considered finance to be like blood supply to the body, (figuratively, the Nation). Blood by itself has no dynamic qualities, it's just a red liquid, but when it moves it takes energy, nutrition and oxygen to the vital parts of the body, collecting the waste material and taking it back to the cleansing organ, the liver and the kidney. This is exactly what finance does to a nation. Just as blood has to move, finance has to move. It has to move forward and get used in something which flourishes, which in turn creates an all round growth.

And just as bad blood is re-circulated after cleaning up, finance needs to be re structured to become healthier for a country. This core concept was helpful in my understanding, not only of the economy, but also of the movement of the stock markets.

Stock exchanges help channelize savings into productive capital. They collect money from those who have saved it and lend it to companies, who in turn manufacture products or offer services to make profits and share it in the ratio with those who have invested in them.

Companies allow people, unknown to each other, to become partners and invest their money in pursuits of future profits. The unit of share in profit is called a 'share' in our day to day terminology.

Stock exchanges had their genesis in Europe, because companies were set up there initially. Later on, Indians also started forming companies under British rule.

There are two types of markets that a Stock Exchange regulates. One, when there is an initial collection of money by a company, which wants to raise money. The people who are invited to invest are given shares; this is called an Initial Public Offering or IPO. Stock exchanges also allow trading in the shares of the company, long after company has collected the initial money, and when someone sells their share of that company to another person, it is called secondary market. Both these activities take place in Stock Exchanges.

Markets work basically on two instruments – 'Debt' and 'Equities'.

Equity is, when you invest in stock and shares of a company, you become a partner, equivalent to the capacity of your investment with them and are therefore entitled to a part of the gain or loss of the company. So it's crucial that you invest in a company which promises good performance and has good future potential, so that you can earn profits.

In case of Debt, you just lend money to the company and they commit to pay you an interest regularly, with a fixed term, to repay the monies you lent. You get your interest regularly and the principal monies you had loaned, when the term expires. However, it does so happen if these companies you loaned monies have performed badly, they neither pay interest nor repay the loaned amount.

As I kept reading, I realised some interesting aspects of how the financial markets do not follow a pattern theoretically structured in economies. In fact they follow a completely different pattern.

Stocks and stock markets are all about demand and supply of money. Understanding this phenomenon, and being able to grasp the nuances, was a skill-set which came to me effortlessly.

By joining IDBI in 1991, I got an opportunity not only to study more about finance but also to observe the stock market at very close quarters. Of course I too had started investing in shares by then.

This was the time when prices and volatility in the market was artificially boosted by Mr. Harshad Mehta. Unfolding of this scam affected thousands of investors who suddenly faced huge losses. This affected me too. In a lighter vein, perhaps I learnt more about markets because I lost a lot of money! And as they say failure teaches more than success, it proved true in my case.

Though I had an interest in stocks, I had no interest in joining the Stock Exchange, as I was in a bank and growing within. But since one of my colleagues quit being a banker and joined the stock market, his connect kept me in touch with the markets.

This bent towards learning about stocks and stock markets was perhaps a precognitive plan that would suddenly materialise into a career! But there were many bridges to cross. A new opportunity fell into my lap.

IDBI was chosen as the lead organisation to set up a modern Exchange called the National Stock Exchange after the Harshad Mehta scam. A team of five people was selected to set it up. Being a junior, I was nowhere in the picture, but one designated officer opted out as he felt this wouldn't succeed, and I became the next choice, the youngest of the entire lot!

The advantages they saw in me was being a gujarati, I could speak with the stock brokers, then my proficiency in technology, especially computers, added to which was my engineering background. I was the only engineer in the five member team. Prima facie these advantages were good enough, however little was I aware that I was embarking on a journey over rough waters!

Had it not been ordained, I could have never learned so much in areas like leasing office place, working with architects, doing interiors, handling licensing procedures, dealing with international companies, handling custom formalities etc. etc. It was like a walk in a labyrinth!

It was a 'touch and go' situation at many junctures. We were attempting to set up something that had no precedent, so there was nothing to fall back upon with absolutely no guidelines to follow!

Let me first give you the background why NSE was initiated.

The first stock exchange in India was set up in 1875, now known as the BSE or Bombay Stock Exchange. Given the nature of business and old traditions, the people who specialized in this trading, didn't allow outsiders to become members of this exclusive club.

BSE was the only place in Mumbai authorized to allow trading in shares. Everyone had to trade through the members of the exchange, by law. The traders would charge brokerage for providing this service to their clients. They had to also abide by rules and regulations of the exchange, laid out and operated by Board of Directors, who were all brokers, appointed through an election procedure. They did employ professionals to execute what the Board of Directors would decide. It was like a Guild of old Europe.

After BSE, many cities asked for Stock Exchanges and were granted permission by the government. There were 22 exchanges in different cities by 1991. Delhi, Kolkata, Ahmedabad, Chennai, Bangalore, Cochin, Vadodara, Kanpur, Patna, Ludhiana, Hyderabad and several others. BSE remained the largest exchange on many counts from 1875 to 1991.

Trouble had started brewing for BSE in early 90's. There were allegations that some of these stock brokers, who were members of the exchanges, were indulging in unfair trade practices vis-a-vis their clients and were sometimes cheating them. These practices were prevalent in almost all stock exchanges, owned and operated by stock brokers.

During 1991-92, this conflict of interest, brokers acting both as players and as umpires, while running the Stock Exchanges, became apparent during the Harshad Mehta scam. It was a scam that had to do more with banking, a 'banking plus broking' scandal.

The scam became a clarion call for the Government. Stock Exchanges have to play a more important role in Indian economy. But as was observed by several committees, before 1991 and after 1991, the conflict of interest of regulated players having to regulate themselves – which meant 'self regulation', was not working out.

The solution came from Pherwani Committee, which recommended a new Exchange, which would primarily deal with the debt market, and stock brokers were not to be part of the management of that exchange. It was supposed to be a model Exchange run by professionals, setting standards for others to follow.

Based on this recommendation, the Government mooted the idea of setting up of a Nationwide Exchange, using latest computer technology, which will not have any interference by stock brokers in either decision making or management. The Stock brokers would only have the right to trade, but not manage its functioning, a novel concept in the history of stock exchanges!

The blueprint for the proposed exchange, to be called the National Stock Exchange (NSE), was laid out. Other key elements in the new set up were that it had to be an 'order-driven' system rather than a 'market maker' one in order to boost liquidity, and to ensure, so to speak, 'one order book' for the nation. The team also decided to go in for transparent, screen-based trading; a move which presented further challenges like national telecom connectivity and major changes in the rules of governance.

IDBI wanted NSE to be a dynamic entity, an enterprise with a very modern set up. So it was decided that the entire team of NSE should immediately move out of the IDBI premises and have its own premises.

The hunt for new premises began, and none of my team members were interested in a mundane task like this, so I was instructed by Dr Patil, Managing Director, to go and meet people and obtain a lease for a suitable office premises. In those days, office premises in Mumbai needed to have a commercial licence to function, and it was not an easy task to get such a large office space.

We had almost finalised a place at Paragon Textiles, Lower Parel, but at the last minute they failed to get a commercial licence, so the hunt began again. We finally got a place at Mahindra Towers, Worli. The management decided to give the interior designing to a young architect, so that delivery time frames could be ensured. Sudhir Dewan was entrusted with the job, and I was appointed the nodal officer to work with him.

During this phase I got introduced to a new aspect of expertise, doing up interiors of an office! And this was an added responsibility along with working on technology! Multiple responsibilities meant constant supervision, so I was compelled to sleep in the office or some nearby premises, eating at small food outlets, which still exist! Thank god I had no family in the city, during those days.

While setting up of our new office, we were putting up a LAN network, which was a new concept that time.NSE had a senior person, who had lots of experience in IT.

Though I was senior to him in hierarchy, academically or experience wise I had no IT background as such. I decided to order 'thick wire' for LAN connections, since I had read that it was recently introduced in the market.

The prevailing system was to use 'thin wire', which was a lot of thin strands bound by an outer cover, whereas the thick wire had just one single cable, with a plastic coating. This 'thick wire' was akin to what was used in cable TV connections. All the seniors opined that I had made a major blunder in ordering thick wire, and that it would fail.

The wire came, we installed them and the system worked! This was a perfect example of how sometimes a long experience creates a rigidity to adapt to new technologies, because such people carry a baggage of what they have learnt and have put to use over and over again. In contrast, inexperienced younger people, who don't carry any baggage, adapt easily to technological changes.

The first step for the new Exchange was to set up an internal as well as an external telecom network, which had to be through leased lines. NSE was mandated to streamline the wholesale debt market, by removing irregularities, through telecom connectivity.

The leased lines were costly. Each line would cost around ₹ 0.4 Million per annum as rentals, within Mumbai for a 64 kbps speed. However, since the wholesale market was booming, we had over a 100 stock brokers who were ready to pay that much money.

Telecom was under Government control. BSNL was the only authority and we at NSE, would become the first private body to have used a private telecom network, a concept called Closed User Group or CUG. This implied that we needed to take a series of approvals, procure licences and do loads of paperwork. This became a part of the National Budget too.

So at one end I was working on interiors, at another attending to all the licensing procedures and also handling the smooth functioning of leased lines. Those days the leased line operators were very unreliable. So we had to be on our toes to monitor them to prevent breakdowns.

The Telecom set up that we had in India at that time was very poor. A telephone connection would take years to get installed and a leased line between two cities would cost millions of rupees per year, with very little reliability. Data connectivity across computers, within cities and outside, was even more unreliable and slow. We had to find a solution, if we had to achieve this dream!

The real time data collection exercise that I had chosen for the B .Tech project became instrumental in my ability to adapt technology in this situation. This became an invaluable experience for me, henceforth.

In 1993, India had already achieved a huge breakthrough with the setting up of the computerised Railway reservation system. By then, even companies like TCS started bagging international contracts in the IT sector.

Yet, Information Technology at that time was still at a very nascent stage in India, not very popular. But the initiative of setting up NSE had the potential to change the horizon of IT in our country and when we commenced working on it, I realised that we had the best of people to take up this challenge.

I put forward a new idea which was to use 'satellite connectivity'. Using a satellite meant that there would be no need of laying physical cables for telephony. India by then had launched satellites, but unlike other countries, we were using them for research and not for commercial operations.

My concept was that satellite communication network for NSE would bring India onto a single platform. A single nationwide order book was unheard of, we were poised to venture into something no one had even dreamt of. Most importantly, everyone in India would get the same response time of less than two seconds.

Most of the people involved believed it to be a pipe dream and that the entire project would fail! And we, from IDBI, being perceived as bankers, were at a disadvantage with no experience in either IT or Telecom or Stock Markets, which was a major minus point for us.

Telecom was also a completely new area for me, so I began reading a lot of books. As always reading was my saviour, to gain self knowledge in a new sector.

For the set up, we had taken the help of a boutique Consultancy Firm, called 'International Securities Consultants'(ISC) Hong Kong, as they were also connected with the London Stock Exchange and had an excellent IT team.

The proposal of using two way satellite communications, made us the first private sector organisation in India to do so, and as usual it was with a lot of resistance.

By this time television channels were also using satellites for telecasting their programmes, which was a one way satellite communication. We were to use satellite communication for sending and receiving information and hence required a technology which was never used in India earlier.

The SATCOM operations and its viability would take time, as we were proposing a radically new idea. All these activities were first of their kind in the country, every stage needing approvals.

In the meantime, our relentless efforts succeeded and the NSE wholesale debt market was ready for its launch, through the LAN and leased line network. We had started trading on NSE several months before the inauguration, to avoid any glitch happening during the inauguration.

The inauguration was on July 23, 1994 at the Nehru Auditorium, the then Finance Minister, Dr. Manmohan Singh was our Chief Guest.

On that day, suddenly Manmohanji landed up at 7.30 am at the NSE office. Luckily a few of us were there, working for the event. On asking him about his early arrival, he said he had nothing to do in the Government guest house, so thought of coming over to check out the systems that we planned to set up!

It was an honour for me to explain the details of our working to make this project a success, from technology, to processing, to cost, to construction and resolution. This has been one of my most memorable moments with the Finance Minister of India, who later became the Prime Minister of India for a period of 10 years.

For SATCOM, we commenced negotiating with several companies to purchase the antennas for setting up two way communication connections via satellite; it had to be a two way interface. During that phase, we realised that if we purchased in bulk, the cost per antenna and electronics came down from ₹ 10 Million per installation, to ₹ 0.5 Million per installation. For the antenna suppliers, the more the quantity, the lesser the cost per antenna. This was because the development cost got amortised with larger numbers. So we decided to buy antennas in large numbers. From an initial number of 50, I negotiated the price for 750 in phase 1.

 The increased numbers implied setting up antennas at many sites and for each site there were hordes of permissions to be taken! A humongous task!

Then to our dismay, we realised that we were given a telecom frequency bandwidth not used anywhere in the world! In spite of this drawback, we fortunately did manage to put this so called 'useless' bandwidth to good use.

Since childhood I was able to do my duties without any complaints, despite all odds. Very early in life I had realised that life is not fair in reality and within this unfair life and society you have to strive to make it meaningful and achieve results.

I was never disheartened or dissatisfied with setbacks, in fact these setbacks pushed me to work even harder and achieve results. This small victory was a reconfirmation of my faith.

It was time for us to select a vendor to create the complete set up by integrating Telecom with IT software /hardware. We wanted to deal with only one entity, who would integrate both of these seamlessly, to make handling easier.

In the course of our research, we realised that these two aspects had to be treated separately, as they were two completely different domains. So we chose to appoint a consortium for each, to collaboratively work towards making the plan a success. And so TCS, Tata Consultancy Services were selected for software, as they had tied up with TCAM, which had created software for Vancouver Stock Exchange. HCL, Hindustan Computers Limited was selected to head the consortium of telecom side.

It was an intense phase of work, work and more work. We were initiating and trying to execute radically new concepts and new ideas, and still had to function within the massive framework of protocols!

While implementing NSE, I was working 15 - 16 hours a day, rarely with any weekend breaks. NSE had given me an apartment at Vile Parle for 4 years, but I hardly visited the apartment, except to sleep and have a bath.

On one holiday for the Holi festival, I came out of my apartment at 11 am to go for breakfast at nearby Udipi restaurant, my neighbour's son was seated outside his apartment with colours in his hands. He looked at me with complete surprise and asked me whether I really came out of my apartment?

I told him yes. He almost scolded me "how can you do that? No one stays there." I was taken aback, but understood his problem and explained to him 'Son, I stay in this apartment but leave for work before you wake up and come back late, when you are fast asleep." My answer still couldn't convince him about the truth!

Once we decided to set up satellite telecom network, with screen based trading, R F P's were issued. We had to scan through profiles of over 60 agencies to evaluate their bids and that required me to travel to the US. But, since I was very young and a bachelor, my US visa was rejected, added to this disadvantage was that by this time my family had migrated there. I was therefore deemed as a potential migrant by the US authorities.

After 3 to 4 rounds of rejections, my Chairman, Mr S. S. Nadkarni, personally talked to the US Ambassador, and made me put in my visa request again, that too got rejected!. Then he issued a personal guarantee that I would return to India, which worked and ultimately I got my visa.

The US Visa officer couldn't believe that a young officer of 24-25 years of age could take such important decisions involving huge amounts of money and it was only this man, who could make the project work. The vendors who had submitted the bids had also got their Senators and Congressmen to write to Mumbai Visa Office requesting issuance of my visa. This level of co operation and spirit fascinated me! The American system works in favour of business, without hiding anything.

If the same had happened for sale of Indian technology by an Indian company, I doubt whether anyone in Indian Government would have taken a similar call to help private technology companies.

As a 25 year old, the immense trust of my Chairman, giving me complete authority to negotiate huge business deals was a big boost for me. This was not for my ego, but as an opportunity to prove that I would fulfil my duties with integrity, increasing my confidence tenfold.

Perhaps such gestures are very important by seniors, to be able to see the potential in a junior and allow him or her complete freedom, which invariably works out in the best interest of the organisation.

Mr. Nadkarni also told me that on my return I must meet the Visa Officer, not only to thank him, but also to prove a point, that it was a business trip. As he suggested, I did meet the Visa issuing officer on my return and could feel his embarrassment of misjudging me to be an illegal migrant. After this incidence NSE never faced visa rejection from the US Embassy.

GTE Spacenet of USA (now Verizon) was finalised as our hub supplier.

The satellite equipment was shipped to India and landed at our customs. Another shock came in the form of a sudden strike at the customs, at a crucial time, and it was a long strike lasting more than 50 days!

Here we were all keyed to set up, and the equipment was idling in the customs warehouse! The team of professionals, who had flown from foreign countries, were idling too! These professionals were very strong built due to their nature of work, so alike WWF wrestlers, tall and with bulging biceps, triceps and all muscles!

After days of waiting, these professionals came to know that Surat, close to Mumbai, was reeling under 'plague'. Scared of this disease, they wanted to go back immediately.

I used to work and sleep in the office during this period on most days. One night these professionals came to me at 3 am, insisting that they had to go back. I was in a tight spot. We were working on a major project and if they went back, it would be chaos. On the spur of the moment I casually asked them for their passports, and as soon as they handed them to me I took them, put them in my cupboard and locked it, an action that became a firm statement 'No, you can't go!'. I was a puny little guy, as compared to these strong Americans, but they were polite and went back.

It was now the turn of their superiors to intervene and they sent an ultimatum to get the equipment out in seven days or they return. We went running to customs officials, pleaded, explained the situation and requested them to release the equipment. Fortunately they agreed on the condition that we pay the duties once the strike was over. We were allowed to take the equipment out, given the national importance of the project.

Another stumbling block was overcome, but problems continued.

After a few months of successfully running the wholesale debt markets, the scenario changed, and the markets slowed down. So it was decided that we now begin working on the Nationwide Equities market, for which we had assumed that we had a time frame of over a year or more, if at all we were to launch it. Dr Patil decided to launch it on Diwali day, November 3, 1994, just three months away! He had reasons for deciding this date, but never revealed it to us.

So we were challenged again. It was now scheduled to be fully functional in the next couple of months! We went running to TCS, our prime software consultants, but they needed 18 months to give us the new software!

I decided with my team that we adapt the software used for wholesale trading and carry out minor modifications to make it suitable for equities.

At 4 am on November 3, 1994, the day of commissioning, I was at the airport to pick up the Indian origin specialist from USA Mr. Karamchand. From the airport we drove straight to NSE and he began to work on the connections. To our greatest surprise and joy, by lunch time the first VSAT became live! It was nothing less than a miracle! We had not planned VSATS to go live, due to paucity of time and risks involved! We expected that just the 104 terminals on LAN at NSE office would get connected; instead approximately 20 VSATs and 1000 leased lines also started working!

The Equities market at the National Stock Exchange was up! The nation's first automated Exchange, neither owned nor managed by member brokers, was going live in the evening for 'muhurat' trading in the evening on 3rd November 1994.

The success of NSE was a first major achievement in the history of Stock Exchanges in the world and the harbinger of taking IT to the next level. The NYSE, NASDAQ and other exchanges followed suit.

About 104 terminals were installed at the NSE offices when the trading commenced.

On the first day there was great excitement among the people who were available. Each one wanted to be the first to trade. Among them was a young trader, Santosh Biyani, who in his over enthusiasm, traded in Reliance shares, but by mistake punched in ₹ 100 above the price. Within minutes, he faced a huge loss.

Now, this was an online trade, unlike the conventional trading floor, where you can see the person whom you trade with. Santosh got panicky and came running to us, as we were trading from NSE office itself. We sympathised with him as it was a genuine mistake. But the challenge on this new platform was that we didn't know the buyer! With great efforts, we went into the back end and traced the buyer, a large and reputed house, whom we pleaded with and who gracefully reversed the transaction. Khandwala Securities, who were trading from their office agreed to let go of a huge profit on the first trade!

I empathised with Santosh most, because with my monthly salary of ₹ 3000/- when a young trader loses millions of rupees in a jiffy, it was like losing a fortune. It was fortunate that he got back his amount, but this was an unforgettable incident for us, because we were made to trace someone, on a platform where buyers and sellers are unknown and faceless!

There was an old veteran aged almost 70, Mr. R D Shah, a legend on the BSE floor, who I noticed was coming from the very first day at NSE. Every day he would come with a young boy, who would sit on the PC and conduct transactions as per the old man's instructions. After five to six days of observation, I went up to him and asked, "Kaka, why do you come here every day"?

He said, "I only know the mechanics of trading, but the speed and facility that you have given is beyond what I could imagine and so I get this boy with me, who understands the computer related aspects of online trading. At my age I can't move around on BSE floor and hence I like it here". The winds of change were blowing, and in that process even the older generation began to accept online trading as a way of life. Mr. R D Shah used to conduct over a hundred trades at NSE daily, a speed that showed a veterans strength.

What began with very few trades initially, gradually picked up high speed, 'Online trading' became a buzz word. Brokers started setting up terminals outside Mumbai, the first being in Coimbatore in 1995, by one Mr. Balasundaram. I went for the inauguration function and observed that it was a huge achievement for them. His old father still couldn't accept the fact that one could trade through a computer and confirmation came in within 2 seconds. He thought I was fooling him!

Some of the brokers even thought that it was some sort of a magic. This success was a giant stride for our country; 'Speed' got a new definition in an age old practice!

Within eleven months, the new stock exchange equalled the daily turnover of its rival, the BSE. By the time the NSE completed a year, it had surpassed the BSE, and after 18 months, its daily turnover had surged to one-and-a-half times that of the older Exchange.

The pioneering move of using satellite network for communication initiated the setting up of ATM's at a rapid pace all over the country. Most of the Banks started using the same software, successfully proven at the NSE.

Satellite connectivity was a boon to create central databases and core banking. Indian banking was catapulted in to 'hi tech' domain. New banks like HDFC bank and old institutions like ICICI, who adopted the new technology, became the largest banks in India over a short period of 20 years.

What we consider today as a necessity was looked upon as a dream and impractical at that point of time!

Despite the success of technology implementation, NSE's business success was not guaranteed. For the first few months it didn't trade as much as we had envisaged, thankfully the much needed boost came from another source.

In mid 1995, the BSE suddenly banned trading in Reliance shares, due to some controversy. At that time a team of about eight people, all Company Secretaries from the Reliance Group of Companies, came to check us out and observe our operations at NSE.

Post their visit, applications from all Reliance companies arrived on my table on the same day. At that time I was also in charge of listing of companies and had to consult my boss, Dr Patil, whether to accept the applications of these companies or not, as Reliance was going through some controversy. My boss in turn told me, "You take your decision, don't send this for approval."

I was a mere 25 year old boy. I took the positive decision at my own risk with reasoning that if they have come to NSE, it was my duty to accept them.

This became a turning point for the NSE. Within few months 80,000 transactions per day took place only of Reliance Companies. Volumes galloped multi-fold.

As a revenue model NSE used to charge a small amount per transaction. At that time we had calculated that if NSE does some 10,000 transactions in a day, it will be sufficient to survive. Today, NSE transacts more than a 10 Million transactions per day.

When NSE started trading in equities from November 3, 1994, an acute need was felt to develop NSE's own equity index, as most large exchanges in India had their own indexes. NSE started with 'Top 200' stocks in market capitalization from other exchanges on 'permitted to trade' basis without listing them.

I quickly created an index called 'NSE 100' taking the top 100 out of the stocks getting traded on NSE. It was calculated real time and disseminated on NSE trading terminals called 'NEAT' terminals from November 22, 1994. NEAT terminals in equities were developed under my leadership and training for brokers commenced, initially within NSE premises and later in different cities.

This phase for me was full of heavy responsibilities. My hands were full, I was involved with multiple aspects, screen based trading, market operations, clearing and settlement, surveillance, regulations, sales, marketing, information technology, construction etc.

Right from the inception the team members handling procurement and construction activities, including interior decoration of offices were reporting to me. The first office at Mahindra Towers, Worli, and then the Kala Ghoda Clearinghouse House, Kamala Mills Clearing house, NSDL premises in Kamala Mills and the new building of NSE at BKC etc. came up under my supervision in addition to most state offices.

We conceptualised the National Securities Clearing Corporation (NSCCL) and was part of the initial set up of the National Securities Depository Limited (NSDL).

For all these activities I felt accountable and answerable, without any expectations of rewards. The fructification of a dream with a long term vision was an ample reward for me.

There was no ambition of a desiring position or money driving me. I was so like a monk, with no desire to accumulate or amass wealth. I took my work to be my enjoyment. Whatever came my way, I gave it more than 100%.

This phase taught me to be confident and not to feel inferior. Even the best and brightest I have met, across the world in several different fields till date, are normal human beings who need empathy. Empathy and sympathy have helped me connect well with both the rich and the poor. I never tried to sweeten my talks to pamper any one, and am always keen to help others at any level.

In the same year, some of us from finance industry were sent to Washington DC on US AID training program for 15 days. The program was organized by an agency called INTRADOS. During the program, we had to introduce each other to other participants.

I was 28, single and had no girlfriend. Hearing this, one of the lady participants asked me why so. I had no answer.

I told her, "I like my work and I am so busy that I didn't have time to have any stable relationship in Mumbai where I work."

However, the pressure to get married was increasing due to increasing age. I believed that it would be impractical, who would want to marry me? I was not interested in worldly things. Most of my salary was spent in buying books or hosting friends. There were no savings and no thought about the future!

An unusual experience at this point of time came to my rescue, an awakening of sorts!

I had been interested in Buddhism and its philosophy of 'No God' and concepts of karma, reincarnation, eight fold paths etc. Due to constant nagging by a friend who would regularly do 'Vipasana,' I agreed to go for the first time to do Vipasana at Igatpuri.

It was a 10 day program where you are not allowed to talk to anyone, can't use phone or newspapers, you just meditate from early morning to late evening. In the evening, Pujya Goenka ji, the founder of Vipasana foundation would personally give his discourses.

Vipasana was a life changing experience it solved my personal quest related issues and calmed my mind substantially.

COIMBATORE STOCK BROKERS
NSE TRADING INAUGURATION
12·7·1995
The Future of
Indian Debt Market '98
Commodities:
The next step
BAMS
The Business Area markets Series
BUSINESS
ICICImarkets.com
THE INDIAN EQUITY MARKET AFTER JULY 02
The 5th Annual Invest India
Securities Industry Summit, 2001
india
REUTERS
IBM

STHITAPRAGYA

Chapter 7

A New Galaxy .... *launch of Derivatives and multi tasking
for Reliance Group of Companies (1995 - 2009)*

*'Knowledge is better than practice; meditation is better
than knowledge; and best of all is surrender, which soon
brings peace.'*

Bhagwad Geeta

At NSE, I was in charge of several activities like technology, equities market derivatives, indexes, membership, listing, premises, administration etc. Towards the end of 1995, I was informed that people were being hired to head the IT and Equities trading at NSE!

I sort of became jobless. With a small salary at that time and no reserves, I felt that I was facing a blind curve.

In just 11 months NSE became larger than BSE. Ironically, success always draws many claimants, a very common phenomenon in large organisations. The dedicated people who worked to create the foundation are obliterated, it's the superstructure that dazzles, but the core is not seen.

Asked by my seniors what would I desire to take up next, I told them I would love to make finance and markets as a career.

Late 1995, there was a new buzz word in the financial sector in India, 'Derivatives'.

I was told to begin work on formulation and execution of derivatives. It was perhaps a ploy to ease me out of core functioning of NSE Equity markets and IT, as both were functioning smoothly by then. Co incidentally within just a month or two the newly appointed senior officer, who was heading Equities, was not able to manage, and that portfolio came back to me.

In December 1995, I wrote the first letter to the Executive Director of SEBI, Mr. O.P. Gaharotra, requesting an approval for commencing derivatives market in India.

From 1997, in order to create more and more awareness, I started lecturing on Derivatives at Management Institutes like S P Jain, Somaiya etc. This being a new concept, I had to explain the complete framework to the students. I structured my own courses, set the syllabus and over the next five years spent countless hours in lecturing at Institutes all over India.

The term 'Derivative' means 'by product', something derived from something else. For example, oil is a derivative of ground nut, but that's not the only derivative of a ground nut, it also offers the husk and the cake, left after extracting the oil. So we have three derivatives from one item, and the prices of all three depend on that of the groundnut! Derivatives have no price of their own. They are dependent on the price of the material they have been derived from.

In financial markets, derivatives have a very interesting usage. You actually create a contract with the trend of changing prices. For example if the price of a Sensex is ₹ 41,000 today, but if you have to buy it after one month, it will not be the same, and so the price will keep varying if the term is after three months or three years.

The current price is called the 'Spot' price, but if you enter into a contract for future, this current price becomes the 'Underlying' price.

Now if you want to buy after one month and you have a contract with somebody, either a bank or broker, that contract is a derivative of the Sensex price today.

There are two types of derivatives; one is Forward, which means 'in the future' and the other is Options, which means, 'if I feel like buying I will opt for it, otherwise not.' The buyer has that choice.

Forward contracts are very common in our day to day life too. Let me give you an example. If you need gold after six months, for your daughter's wedding, you will want to buy gold after six months. If currently gold is available at ₹ 28,000 per ten grams, and someone is offering to give it to you for ₹ 29,000 after six months, you enter into a 'forward' contract with him.

If after two months, the gold price has gone up to say ₹ 30, 000, your contract will also go up in value, because the underlying price has gone up.

That ₹ 29,000, you had promised to buy at, would be valued at ₹ 31,000. Now, because you have signed an agreement with you supplier, he is bound to give you gold at ₹ 29,000, which becomes your profit.

But if this was an Options contract, then you have a choice to buy it at ₹ 29000 or not to buy it at all. Here, one person has a choice, the other doesn't. If you decide to buy it at ₹ 29000 he has to sell it, but if you do not want to buy, there is the premium to it.

A life insurance policy is an ideal example of a real life Options contract. You pay a premium for one year and if you want to discontinue, the one year premium you paid for, is forfeited. If you continue, you will get the benefit. Similarly, in our day to day life we use many Options contracts, like booking tickets for trains or airlines, you either use the ticket or cancel them, and the cancellation charges are what you forgo.

While planning to set up the Derivatives Market, we identified several pre requisites. Software for trading derivatives was one of them. Legal changes were required to allow trading in derivatives and index derivatives. Qualified professionals needed to be certified in derivatives. A new index focused on liquidity, to enhance arbitrage between equity and derivatives in index, was also to be developed.

We started working on many such areas simultaneously. Derivatives were a new and dangerous concept from the perspective of the regulators, media and general public. Warren Buffet, the legendary investor had called derivatives as weapons of mass destruction. Barings Bank, the oldest bank in the world, had collapsed with use of exchange traded derivatives in Singapore, in 1994.

Moreover, reading the literature and books on derivatives, people came to conclusion that only highly qualified people in mathematics would be able to do it and it was not meant for general public in India. No one in India wanted to teach derivatives. 'Black Scholes' formula and 'John Hull' books on derivatives had created a very difficult scenario. A majority of people were reluctant to even talk about complex mathematics involved!

Software vendors who had never thought about derivatives had convinced the seniors at NSE to buy new and extremely expensive software from a European Exchange, which had just come up. The cost would have been in the range of USD 100 million, if all things were to be taken in to account. All software's from Europe were working on different communications protocols and screens. Indian traders had got used to NSE NEAT interface. I had to think through and convince the seniors and NSE Board about the futility of buying expensive software, which might not be easy to implement and could take a long time to modify before commencing operations.

Software vendors were also marketing their tie ups. I was told that I was not an expert on derivatives and that the experts were saying that current software would not work. Several foreign experts were coming to make presentations to NSE to convince them to buy their software.

Finally, I hired two experts who had some knowledge of derivatives. We visited all places in Europe where new automated derivatives exchanges were coming up. After a trip of one week along with experts and other colleagues, a report was submitted that it will be advisable for NSE to use its current software, with required modifications.

I convinced the Board and seniors to let me try the modification of the existing NEAT software and prepare back office, clearing and settlement, risk management and other software along with regulations for the derivatives segment. I was allowed to do that because no one believed that derivatives trading will ever be allowed in India and even if it was allowed, I will not be able to make it work, because I had never traded in derivatives markets before. My team and I started working on various aspects. We divided the team and each team took up a focussed activity.

We also set up NSE's certification in financial markets, a completely automated exam system for taking derivatives certifications exams. We started equities and depository exams. The curriculum was set, books were prepared and made available on the NSE website to be downloaded. A lot of people started taking these screen based exams. It was a very hectic period.

The task was difficult because I had to create awareness among people across the country. I would book a large hall in a city or a town and advertise in local newspapers about a 'Seminar on Stock Market and Derivatives'. We also had to advertise that dinner /lunch would be provided and a few free gifts will be given away for good questions. This initiative met with a lot of success even in the remotest corners of India. From 1996 to 2000, I must have spoken about derivatives in simple Hindi and English in over 400 Conferences, Seminars, Colleges etc. pan India, a record of sorts!

A new index had to be created which allowed for more liquidity. We had some data of trading in equities by then. We took help in calculations from the young faculty at IGIDR, Dr. Ajay Shah and Dr. Susan Thomas, who were my seniors from IIT. They were good at data crunching. I would spend my weekends at IGIDR, Goregaon, Mumbai explaining to them how markets worked and other details. We ended up doing very large number of calculations, using several million portfolios, to also ensure that the index would be useful for hedging of most portfolios in the economy.

After complete analysis, the IGIDR team suggested an index, which would cover 66% of India's market capitalization and variable number of companies, in that index. I had gone through many rounds of discussions and had to suggest a fixed number of stocks, which was also easy to remember. I had figured that the world was not ready for a variable number of companies in an index, irrespective of what the theoreticians felt. There was a slight difference between pure idealistic theory and practical reality.

Finally, 'NSE 50' was born, with 50 companies. The 'NSE 50' or Nifty index started getting published. I was called by Mr. Gaharotra of SEBI and informed to change the name of the index from 'Nifty 50' to something else because 'Nifty 50' had a very bad reputation in US. It seems he had got a feedback that there were 'Nifty 50' companies in 1960s in US which failed miserably and hence it may happen to the new index too. We had good amount of arguments and finally decided to wait, before taking any final decision.

'NIFTY' Index', the most traded index in derivatives in India today, was launched on 21st April 1996 .The full form of 'NIFTY' is 'National Stock Exchange Fifty'. It represents the weighted average of 50 Indian company stocks in thirteen sectors of the Indian economy and offers investment managers exposure to the Indian market in one portfolio. It is one of the two main stock indices used in India.

I got married in 1998. Since my wife, Sonal, was in the final year of her medical studies at Ahmedabad, post marriage she continued studying for a year and joined me in Mumbai in late 1999.

By 1999, there were indications that Dr Patil would retire in a year. So I decided to quit NSE, apply for a job at the World Bank, and if I got it, go to the USA. The World Bank authorities called me for a final interview to Japan, but I didn't get the job under the Young Professionals (YP) program of World Bank.

In 2000 I applied once again. I knew that I had two major drawbacks, no post graduate degree from an International University and no foreign language skills. In spite of these drawbacks, I was called to Washington DC for the final interview.

It was peak winter when I landed there, in February 2000. The entire city was at a standstill, being snowbound for seven days. Having landed there, I was called to the World Bank Head Quarters, but the seniors being absent, someone at the junior level took my interview! And this happened everyday when I went to the World Bank Headquarters.

On the third day, when I was there, I got a call from Mr Manoj Modi, from Reliance Group. He said "we've heard you want to quit the NSE, if you are interested you can start a Petrochemical Exchange for us".

I replied, "If I don't get a job at the World Bank in US, I will come back." It so happened that the job offer I got was not good, and the placement was in India, so I decided to return to India and to accept the offer of Reliance.

At Reliance, I asked for the salary equivalent to what I would have got from World Bank, and they readily agreed.

In 2000, I set up the company 'exchangenext.com' for them, hired around 100 people and started B2B Commerce in Petrochemicals. We also got prepared for starting B2B markets on Paper, Steel and Cement etc. and were looking at corporate bodies to back them.

Sadly in 2001, though internet became popular, the 'e commerce' business came crashing down in India.

Overnight a team of 100 people became jobless, but since we were good at technology, they shifted us all onto the telecom sector, and so we stared work on Reliance Communications Network .There were already thousands of people working on that project at that time.

The rate for mobile telephone calls then was ₹ 16/- per minute. Reliance launched mobile telephony at 20 paise per minute. They offered a mobile connection at ₹ 501 and monthly payment of ₹ 500/- thereafter. This pricing gave them a huge upsurge of buyers, but the billing systems were not well tested. Tracing subscribers was next to impossible, so bills remained unpaid and losses mounted up.

These services were based on a new technology CDMA, and so we used to work through day and night for almost a year. Mr. Mukesh Ambani and Mr. Manoj Modi also used to work with us during those difficult times, late in the nights too!

One night, Mr Mukesh Ambani called me at 2 am and asked me "What does a CIO or Chief Information Officer do? Do we have a job specification for a Telecom CIO? I said, I would find out and revert. I dug out all information to present it to him, the next day. He heard me out about the role and straightaway said "You are the CIO, now clean up the mess". He was just testing me while asking about the CIO job specification.

The challenge was not that frightening , but I was too young and Reliance had many seniors. It would be embarrassing for me to instruct them, so I requested Mr. Mukesh Ambani to inform all of them in writing, otherwise I would have faced resistance. He not only did that, but also gave me complete freedom.

Within six months the billing issue was resolved. We had implemented the streamlining exercise without making the company spend any money on new software. I just tweaked the existing software, as well as used it in another business application process. This achievement made me a hero of IT, though I was not!

The more I wanted to move away from IT, the more it came back to me!

A little after that, both the Ambani brothers split their businesses, and I was now with Reliance Communications, which was with Mr Anil Ambani. They soon appointed a new person as their CIO and I quit the job.

Having got to know that I had left, Mr. Mukesh Ambani asked me to join him. At that time I said "it's OK, I can survive on teaching and unless there is a proper requirement I would not like to come back". Promptly he said, "from now on you would be the CIO of the Reliance

Group'. History repeated itself and once again, I had to request him to inform all the seniors in writing!

Having settled at that position and commenced handling the portfolio, a midnight call from Mr. Mukesh Ambani was with a new proposition "can you additionally handle Media Relations?" This was something new for me, all I could say was "I can try". Overnight I became Head of Media Communications of Reliance Group, in addition to being the Group CIO.

In 2006, we launched Reliance Retail, Reliance Fresh and Reliance Digital.

I managed the Media Relations portfolio till 2008, it was a great experience. Reliance, at that time, was facing many allegations and it was in this phase that a major fire had erupted at their Refinery, so it meant days and nights of trouble shooting.

A de merger of the Group into five companies was planned and since I had the experience of managing a stock exchange, I was called to participate in that activity also.

Reliance Petroleum decided to have an IPO in 2006, in order to gets its shares listed. I had to represent the Company as the senior most officer, to each stock exchange and make a presentation on why the company should be listed.

When I made the presentation to the BSE, the Listing Committee of BSE opined that they would list the shares only if we allowed them to put all the funds in an 'escrow' account and then they would decide how to release funds. Coming from a stock exchange background, I was surprised and asked them "is there any such regulation?" I knew such a rule didn't exist. I also asked them "have you done this for any company earlier?" To both the questions there was no reply!

On asking them 'why' such a condition was being proposed by them for only Reliance Petroleum, their answer was that they were apprehensive of funds being misused! I informed them that this company had a treasury larger than many banks. Having made up my mind not to budge, I politely told them that "I am waiting in the adjoining room. You take your time to decide and let me know". After half an hour, two senior brokers came to my room and told me that they were withdrawing the condition, and granting us permission!

On reporting this to Mr Mukesh Ambani, when I returned in the evening, I was given a pat on my back for having taken the correct decision. Mr Mukesh Ambani gives his people complete authority, along with responsibility, which is very vital for an individual's growth. The key learning is that being accountable makes you more responsible and that makes you want to do your job with complete dedication.

Around this time my ex colleagues from NSE had started a software firm to develop software for stock brokers. My wife was part owner of that company, though she was not software professional. That company grew too big, with almost a 100 employees and needed full time focus and attention. As I was enjoying my work at Reliance, we decided to sell it off. In 2007, we got a buyer, and handed over the company to them.

The Reliance Petroleum IPO, the largest IPO from India in those days, was oversubscribed more than 51 times, over 2.1 Million people subscribed to it! It was an admirable display of faith in a progressive organisation.

The Ambani family works really hard, harder than almost every employee working for them.

In 2008, a new chapter dawned in my life! Cricket came back into my life with a big bang!

One night, around 3 am, I got a call from Mrs Nita Ambani requesting me to meet her in the morning. During that meeting I was informed that Reliance had bought an IPL cricket team 'Mumbai Indians', which was already known to all of us and the first match was scheduled in four days and that I was being made responsible to run 'Mumbai Indians' henceforth! Mr. and Mrs. Ambani knew about my love and passion for cricket.

'Mumbai Indians' had already created a team and all media activities were in full swing. The first match was just four days away and we had not sold a single ticket!

My first job was to just distribute maximum number of tickets for the match at Wankhede stadium. For over two decades, I had been to the Wankhede Stadium to play club cricket matches and also to watch many matches when the Indian cricket team would be playing. Little did I imagine that I would be organizing matches at this venue! At that time Wankhede Stadium was undergoing major repairs. The entire external area was half dug up. Post IPL, it was supposed to be fully demolished, in order to build a brand new stadium for the World Cup in 2011.

Getting 35,000 people to the Wankhede Stadium to watch a three hour match was a huge challenge, especially since we had just four days, which included the day of the match! IPL was a completely new concept. No one had experienced it before.

We had to plan and execute distribution of tickets to reach the right people, and that too very very fast. And we didn't want to distribute the tickets for free, a habit which would set a wrong precedent.

Before the advent of IPL, Mumbai would host an international match once in a few years and most tickets would be sold through the associated clubs without any hassle. Very few tickets were sold at the ticket windows, there being a natural shortage, it was easy to sell tickets for International One Day matches.

In our case, we had to sell tickets for 10 matches comprising 7 home, 2 semi finals, and 1 final, in a short span of 35 days. Each match would last for only three hours, as compared to one day or five day matches hosted earlier. And IPL was not even an International tournament, although it had International cricketers playing for different teams.

We sold the tickets to a large number of Reliance employees. Most of them used to stay at Navi Mumbai as Reliance group has a huge office complex there. We despatched 1000 tickets each to distributors of Reliance products. We also commenced selling tickets through Reliance outlets. 'E selling' was a new concept. Though an agency was selected for sale of tickets, before I joined the team, they were not able to sell many.

Our strategy worked. Within two days, we had sold most tickets to Reliance employees and through the Reliance distributors. It was the human touch that helped. However, as per regulations, 20% of the tickets had to be given free to Mumbai Cricket Association 'MCA' for their consumption. Because of shortage of time, they didn't even send tickets to the associated clubs!

On the day of the first match, I accompanied Mr Mukesh and Mrs Nita Ambani to the stadium. They looked around and were pleased with the attendance. However, one large stretch of stadium, the entire 'Sunil Gavaskar' stand and a few other high cost seats were empty. Mrs Nita Ambani asked me as to why they were not occupied. I informed her that the seats in that area belonged to MCA and those tickets were not even shipped out by them. She said "can we fill that portion of the stadium as well? Can we at least try?" I said, "Let me try."

I went out and asked my colleagues as to where would the tickets be, which were handed over to MCA. To my shock and surprise, they were lying in a corner of the ticket office, untouched and fully packed! I took out a few hundred tickets, went to the Churchgate side ticket window and threw those tickets in the air.

A lot of people were standing around. One of them took hold of the paper flying in the air and shouted "Free match tickets". Within a few seconds there was a commotion. People were grabbing the free tickets and entering the stadium. And I was caught right in the middle of the chaos of people who were jostling for the free tickets! The Police turned up and took me to their van. By this time more tickets had been given out. The Policemen did not allow me to leave the van, despite my protests that I was the head of the Mumbai Indians.

Soon my colleagues from Mumbai Indians security team came and told the police about my position. I was then released, to make further arrangements.

The 'spur of the moment' decision had worked, the stadium was filled to the brim for the first match before it had commenced. Everyone was happy, including the people, who got a surprise gift of a match ticket on that day.

The Mood Indigo (IIT) days had given me ample training.

It worked wonderfully, the event was a success!

After this experience, we planned each match meticulously, including the security, evacuation and other drills in addition to cameras, in ground advertisements and so many other aspects, including the arrangements for practice for the teams, their travel, stay etc etc.

Fuelled by the success of the very first match, our ambitions took wings.

There were nine matches scheduled further, and tickets had to be sold. Worried about the fan fatigue, we had to bring a new set of fans to the grounds. We now focused on families. For them to come, we had to have better seating arrangements. We planned facilities like Multiplex type seat booking with instant confirmations of allotment with better facilities and faster entry and exit etc.

It was a tough arrangement to make. Added to that challenge a new dimension emerged. Another stadium, the D Y Patil stadium in Navi Mumbai was also included, after the first match. But there was a catch, we couldn't know even a week prior to the match as to which stadium the match would be played!

So, we had to keep both Wankhede and D Y Patil stadiums ready. This meant that tickets were to be printed overnight and we just got a couple of days to sell tickets. I and my team had sleepless nights for 45 days, during the series, just to ensure that first season of Mumbai Indians goes smoothly, without a complaint.

During this entire phase, both Mr Nikhil Meswani and Mrs Nita Ambani were always available for discussions on important decisions. After a decision was taken, they left it to me to implement the action. This unique approach and method of selecting the right person and giving him or her complete authority to execute it, is perhaps the reason why Reliance witnesses quick implementation of most of their projects.

I had enjoyed similar authority along with responsibility during the phase when the telecom division had billing problems, which I had to resolve and later on as President and Chief Information Officer of Reliance Group, Head of IPO team for Reliance Petroleum and Head of Media Relations for Reliance Group. A unique culture at Reliance, which I have not seen in any other Indian company, is that the entire organisation works with flexible teams and the authority for a project once entrusted to someone, gets an unstinted support from every person. This eradicates a lot of bureaucratic delays that usually happen in large organizations during the process of decision making as well as in execution.

After the first season got over, we completed all accounting procedures and resumed our normal jobs in our departments. I also assumed that my IPL stint was over and for the next season, the organisation would hire a professional to manage Mumbai Indians full time.

In 2009, the following year, the Government of India decided not to give approvals for IPL to be held in India, due to impending general elections. It was decided by the IPL authorities to hold the IPL matches in South Africa. I was not expecting to do much for the team.

One day after the decision by IPL authorities, Mr Mukesh Ambani called me to his room and asked me "are you ready?" I asked "for what? He said, "Haven't you thought through what to do in South Africa?" I quickly regained my composure and said "I will come back in a few days with details."

I went back to the drawing board, connected to the team members who had worked on the first series of IPL, identified new people with international experience and created a plan and presented it to Mr Ambani.

He gave his go ahead and the entire team, support staff were all off to South Africa. During the tournament series, thousands of guests would be coming from India and other countries, which had to be handled, in addition to security of the team, their stay, their travels and day to day coordination amongst many other aspects. It was over sixty day tour with pre matches being organized in different grounds to acclimatize the team. Shawn Pollock, Jonty Rhodes and others who were part of IPL 1 with Mumbai Indians, also pitched in with their knowledge.

We also had to equip the players with hand warmers, as many matches were played in cold weather conditions, it being end of winter season in South Africa, whilst we had summer in India. I learnt many technical details like the height of the venue above sea level also affected the dip of the ball during catches apart from many more interesting things. One of the most interesting facts I learnt was that no one could predict the nature of the pitch for sure. Even the most experienced players and grounds men could have their predictions going wrong. Teams which created a particular composition, based on the nature of the pitch, were generally taken by surprise.

Overall, the entire tournament was a low scoring tournament for most matches, the reason being the old and highly used pitches. IPL 2 was planned at the end of the cricketing season for South Africa. We could see just about seven to eight cities where the matches were held and also had a firsthand experience of the inequality in the South African society.

Since I was staying with cricketers during this period and also went for breakfast, dinners and lunches with them on most occasions, I had much closer interaction with them in IPL 2 compared to IPL 1.

My family came to South Africa, for a few days, during the matches. As there were hardly any young children around for the Indian contingent, my son Shawn (age 7), went with the Mumbai Indians captain for tosses on to the ground, before the live match, on a few occasions. As a practice, a young fan was allowed to accompany the captains for the toss. Shawn mingled freely with all the players. This was a highlight for all of us, especially for Shawn, which we will cherish for a long time to come.

I remember a humorous incident during one such visit. I was sitting with Mr Harsha Bhogle, a well known Indian Commentator. Harsha was among the very few who had got his hair transplant done. My wife was completely shocked seeing him with full hair, as she had seen him bald earlier. She just couldn't believe that his hair had grown! In trying to convince her, we all had a good laugh. We later also introduced her to the hair transplant doctor.

During this tour I remember an important conversation that threw light on how India had changed the game of Cricket. Tommy Mbangwa, ex Zimbabwe cricketer and commentator, said, "With the success of IPL, these cricketers at a young age get so much money in just 35 days. You Indians have changed the world cricket scene! The money that you give them for just 35 days is something which these cricketers wouldn't have earned during their lifetime in cricket! This has started a new movement and cricketers will now retire early, opting to join IPL and not play for their country."

This actually became a fact, because many cricketers followed this route and stopped playing for their country, especially in Australia. Players like Adam Gilchrist, Matthew Hayden etc. took premature retirement.

India was changing the cricket scenario rapidly. Almost 90% of revenues of any cricketing events came from India and that made our country a dominant force in cricket.

During this tenure, in Johannesburg, on one of the off days, I was invited by a friend for dinner. When I came back around 11 pm, a Gujarati family was waiting for me in the hotel lobby. They had a seventeenyear old girl, paralysed neck down, on a wheel chair who was very keen to meet Sachin Tendulkar. Someone had told them that the only way to meet him was through me, as I was the CEO of the team.

It was a cold wintery night and due to paralysis the girl's body was getting colder and colder. I was frantically trying to locate Sachin, but he was not contactable. In a little while even Zaheer came, and we were putting blanket after blanket on the girl and gave her many cups of tea, to keep her warm.

Around 12:30 midnight, Sachin came. I took him aside and told him about this girl's wish to spend some time with him and he readily agreed, took photos with her and spent half an hour with the family.

As soon as they left, Sachin told me that whenever we were playing in Johannesburg, I should send them complimentary passes and make them sit near the boundary. Thereafter, whenever Sachin played in Johannesburg, he used to go to the boundary and greet them warmly.

Like Sachin, all the boys Harbhajan, Yuvraj, Dhoni, Kohli, Ajinkya Rane, Ashish Nehra, Dhaval Kulkarni, Abhishek Nair are polite to a fault, in spite of so much fame and money that they earn at this young age.

My bonding with most of them has remained intact over the years and they are in regular touch with me for any financial or general advice, whenever they need it.

There was another memorable incident during the South Africa tour. At Johannesburg I found out that there was a BAPS Swami Narayan temple functioning from a church in the city. I visited them and they were delighted. Pujya Pramukh Swamiji called me during the prayer meetings and gave me his blessings. From that day onwards till the time we were there, every single day pure vegetarian food for 40-50 people was sent by the temple to the hotel and served in a separate room. All vegetarians on this tour had a problem in getting good vegetarian food and so for us this gesture was God sent. Within a day or two, as more and more people from the other teams came to know about this delicious food, they flocked to eat this pure vegetarian food.

The South Africa tour had its share of challenges too, mainly logistics. The 'city to city' tour meant transportation of all valuable cricketing kits and accessories, which if we took by flight would turn out to be very expensive. So post every match, the entire luggage would get loaded onto buses and leave for a night long journey to the next venue, whilst the team would fly the next day. This complex logistics planning fortunately worked without any mishap.

I always had a liking for events, and handling IPL was a satisfactory achievement, due to its scale and magnitude. Somewhere destiny had groomed me for this since childhood. From organising VCR film shows to handling events during Mood Indigo at IIT, holding summer camps at IIT hostel etc.

By now my health was in bad shape. I had already developed diabetes early on. Throughout these hectic schedules, I kept trying all types of remedies and one of them was to be only on fruits and juices for six months, a diet that made me lose 15 kgs!

I also suddenly developed acute pain in the soles of my feet, which I assumed was because of my flat foot. The pain was so acute that I feared I would not be able to walk at all for the rest of my life!

Coupled with this physical trauma was the mental stress. The software company I had sold came back to me in 2009, with huge losses, as it was not working out for the buyer. This setback was a financial stress for my family, as almost 100 people were employed, and had now become our responsibility.

After coming back from South Africa, I planned a vacation to Europe, with my family. I had told my family that I would remain seated in the bus as I could not walk much, but they could go and see the tourist spots.

Since I was going to London, the first leg of the journey, Rahul Singhvi, my colleague at Mumbai Indians advised me that I must consult a particular doctor there, as he was very good at treating pains.

So, on touchdown at London, I rushed to see him. He was a Chiropractor and physiotherapist. He told me that my being a vegetarian plus being on a strict diet regime, it was necessary that I eat two bananas every day. Surprised I asked "that's all, no medicines?" He prescribed some pills.

We couldn't buy medicines that evening in London. The following day we were in Belgium and went to a chemist to buy the prescribed medicines. The chemist said that he didn't have those particular ones, but could give us substitutes. Out of curiosity we asked the chemist what the medicines were. To our utter surprise the chemist said they were only multi -vitamins! With my dietary control, to reduce sugar, there was no mineral and vitamin content in my intake, which had created this problem.

The Chiropractor's advice worked miraculously and since then my leg pain has almost gone. I can stand for hours, walk long distances and I now follow a more balanced, of course a vegetarian diet.

We came back from Europe and worked on completing the deal of the sale of shares of the IT Company, which my wife owned partially at that time.

By this time the Wankhede stadium was to be demolished. I was planning to stay back in Reliance, after sale of the company. We decided to do the third IPL at Brabourne Stadium of Cricket Club of India (CCI) and started preparations in advance. I made arrangements with CCI to hire their ground and make necessary changes to match the standards for Mumbai Indians. We also did some testing of ticket sales and management of entry and exit with 'Book My Show' during that period.

In the meantime, the IT Company got sold to BSE at a very low cost, and with a condition that I work for them for at least one year. My wife sold all her shares.

I had to resign from Reliance as I had to work with BSE.

STHITAPRAGYA

Chapter 8

Metamorphosis .....*the radical transformation of BSE (2009 onwards)*

'If one offers to Me with devotion, a leaf, a flower, a fruit, or even water, I delightfully partake of that article offered with love by My devotee in pure consciousness.'

Bhagwad Geeta

Post IIM, having traversed a long and varied career path, I had never imagined that I would be a part of a more than century old reputable institution, my 'Karmakshetra'.

The Bombay Stock Exchange is the oldest stock exchange in Asia. Its history dates back to 1855, when 22 stockbrokers used to gather under a banyan tree in front of Town Hall, Mumbai. The location of these meetings changed many times to accommodate an increasing number of brokers. The group eventually moved to Dalal Street in 1874 and became an official organization known as 'The Native Share & Stock Brokers Association' in 1875.

On August 31, 1957, the BSE became the first stock exchange to be recognized by the Indian Government under the Securities Contracts Regulation Act, 1956. In 1980, the exchange moved to the Phiroze Jeejeebhoy Towers at Dalal Street, Fort, Mumbai.

I was destined to helm an outdated Stock Exchange and transform it into becoming the world's largest and fastest Exchange, with over 5000 listed companies. This task was beyond imagination!

By achieving this humongous task, it proved that if we employ the right technology and develop faith in our team, no dream is impossible to achieve.

On my return from the Europe vacation, BSE offered me the post of a Deputy CEO. Since I had to be with them for at least one year, as per the terms of buying the software company, partially owned by my wife, I agreed. They were interested in setting up Derivatives market and I could have been instrumental in helping them as per their expectations.

I informed Mr Mukesh Ambani about this offer from BSE, but he was skeptical about this. I explained him that once the term was complete, I would get enough money for my retirement. He consented graciously and said that he wouldn't want to come in the way of my future plans.

Within me the spirit of facing a challenge was perhaps the reckoning force that made me agree, and of course destiny was at work throwing surprises at me once again!

The broker community was so sure that I would not leave Reliance and join BSE that they even lay their bets among themselves - for and against. Newspaper articles were written against me and a parliamentary question was also raised, eliciting vested interests.

In early 2009, Mr Madhu Kanann was appointed as the CEO of BSE. He had earlier worked for Merriyll Lynch, Bank of America as well as with NYSE.

When I stepped in as a Deputy CEO, BSE was in crisis. It was facing many accusations and allegations. It hadn't kept pace with changing times, neither in technology nor in attitude. That is the reason their loss was NSE's gain.

They had no new products to offer like derivatives, had lost reputation and had constant troubles with trade unions. Their regulatory systems were flawed and frail, and the quality of human resources was not upgraded. It was indeed the most precarious time for me to function as a deputy CEO.I was set to play a vital role in changing the destiny of a gigantic organisation, which was at its nadir, waiting to be awakened.

We realised that there were 5 major issues for me to tackle – Technology, People, Products, Distribution and Reputation. We wanted to resolve them without any enforcement, we desired the heartfelt involvement of its people, because if they get enthused, the entire process would become faster.

We began to work from grass root level. The first step was to change technology completely, and this became possible because of the skill sets of my company, which they had bought over.

Very slowly, over a period of three years, I started feeling the pulse of this giant getting revitalised, without major disruptions.

Metaphorically, we had opened the closed doors and windows of BSE, and showed them the fast changing world outside their institution. We urged them to evolve and anticipate, and made them realise that they had ignored automation and upgrade it for 15 years!

Miraculously, the change of technology resulted in higher profits at very low cost. Time began to turn around for BSE!

Mr. Madhu Kannan, the then CEO, resigned in 2012.I was made the interim CEO.I was supposed to run the exchange till the time a new CEO was appointed and then leave BSE.

BSE appointed a search committee as per regulations. Initially they were searching for a suitable candidate from an IT company to head BSE. After a search for 7 months, in November 2012, I was appointed as the MD & CEO.

As a very old institution, my first task, as a CEO, was to boost the morale of the people from within, by creating trust, giving them authority with responsibility. I gradually introduced the new way of working. I gained the trust of the employees, because I worked without imposition or coercion.

As we evolved with technology upgradation, the entire environment changed, operating speed increased, their spirits got a boost, and we all co operatively started setting and achieving new goals with renewed vigour. All of us were determined that BSE had to be prepared to usher in tomorrow... today!

BSE provides an efficient and transparent market for trading in equity, debt instruments, equity derivatives, currency derivatives, commodity derivatives, interest rate derivatives, mutual funds and stock lending and borrowing.

Between 2012 and 2017, we launched BSE – SME exchange platform, followed by trading in BRICSMART indices Derivatives, followed by launch of Currency Derivatives, Interest Rate Futures etc.

In March 2012, BSE became the first Exchange in the country to launch a dedicated SME platform for listing of Small and Medium Enterprises (SMEs). The BSE SME segment is the market leader of its kind in India, with about 314 SME's listed, 75 of which have grown and successfully migrated to the main Board of the Exchange.

In March 2014, BSE launched the BSE STAR-MF platform is India's largest digital platform to distribute Mutual Funds and commands a market share of close to 80% among exchange distributed funds. The robustness and seamlessness of BSE STAR MF, along with Swiftness of Distributors query resolution through real time interaction, has created an ideal ecosystem for all stakeholders in the India Mutual Funds Industry. 52% of new investors coming to MF industry is routed through BSE STAR MF.

In April 2014, BSE SME exceeded 1 Billion dollar market capitalisation. By November 2014, the Market capitalisation of BSE listed companies crossed Rs 100 Trillion. Later we became the Best Managed Financial Derivatives Exchange.

By Oct 2015 we triumphed with gaining the reputation of being the fastest exchange in the world, with a response time of 6 microseconds!

A 140 yr old organisation had metamorphosed into a 9 yr old hi tech organisation with systematic changes from within, without any outside force.

The mandate of BSE was to protect investors, which meant that we had to have the highest standards of regulatory compliance, and this is what I insisted on honouring, urging them to follow strict guidelines. We designed BSE's systems and processes to safeguard market integrity, drive the growth of the Indian capital market and stimulate innovation and competition across all market segments.

All appraisals were now performance based. The same people, with a change of mindset, had transformed from low morale to highly confident workforce. Earlier, the turnover at its helm was very high. Nobody continued for more than two to three years and many had taken up the position post retirement which meant that their zeal and enthusiasm to refurbish the system was of least concern.

It takes time to bring in change, but we worked on it patiently, right from its roots. Once the foundation becomes strong, the organisation became robust. We all became become profit oriented, which changed the complacent outlook to a dynamic one.

We needed to pass one more litmus test though! BSE, being corporatized, was not permitted to have an IPO, as it was ordained that stock exchanges can't be listed. Most of the brokers and investors, hoping that there would be an IPO in the future, were in for a rude shock. The employees of BSE had lost face, feeling helpless at their inability to be listed. Many brokers had begun to sell their stakes at low value too.

 It was time to take up the issue. So we began a persistent effort of persuasion with the authorities to grant us the permission. With consistent follow up, backed by performance driven results, we created that 'magic' moment - a final nod was given that we could launch our IPO!

In Jan 2017, when we announced our IPO, an unbelievable response of faith and gratification followed. Our IPO was oversubscribed 51 times! We had over a million applications. The people's overwhelming mandate was a stamp of 'trust and faith' in BSE as an institution. What was lost over decades, was regained in one stroke.

Going through this entire process and working as a team, followed by this victory, was a huge morale booster for all the employees. By this time a lot of professionals had joined us too. They were well experienced and qualified people who had left leading institutions to join us, and though they did not enjoy fat salaries, the prestige of being a BSE employee was high.

We made ourselves future ready with innovative ideas, heralding new opportunities. By revamping BSE, we brought in the entire spectrum of products including equity, currency, interest rate derivatives and commodities under one roof. We created a new decade long road map, keeping ourselves flexible to adapt to emerging market trends

BSE has taken leadership position in setting up Small and Medium Enterprises (SME) Platform, Offer for Sale (OFS), Mutual Funds Distribution through Exchanges, e-IPO etc. Our innovation of Mutual Funds platform, which was an experiment, took off so well that it brought in revenue beyond speculated figures. Today, BSE commands more than 70% market share in these segments.

In June 2013, Shri Narendra Modi, the then Hon'ble Chief Minister of Gujarat had visited BSE and after observing our operations, invited us to Gujarat to set up a Modern Exchange in Gift City, an invitation that created another landmark for BSE.

In 2017, BSE set up the 'India International Exchange Limited' or India INX, India's first international exchange, a wholly owned subsidiary of BSE Limited, in the Gujarat International Finance -Tec City.

The Exchange was inaugurated by Hon'ble Prime Minister of India, Shri Narendra Modi, on Jan 09, 2017 and commenced its operations from Jan 16, 2017. Today, it has crossed a daily average turnover of USD 16.70 Billion.

Operating on an advanced technology platform of EUREX T7, India INX is the fastest in the world, with a turn-around time of 4 micro seconds. It offers a first of its kind single segment approach for all asset classes - equities, currencies, commodities and fixed income securities, providing significant cost advantages to its participants.

When I took over as CEO in 2012 the valuation of BSE was Rs 15 Billion. By 2014, the valuation was close to Rs 44 billion, and when BSE was listed in 2017, the market valuation realized was Rs 64.6 Billion.

BSE provides an efficient and transparent market for trading in equity, debt instruments, equity derivatives, currency derivatives, commodity derivatives, Interest rate derivatives, mutual funds and stock lending and borrowing.

BSE signed MOUs countries like Korea and Abu Dhabi for mutual collaboration for growth and advancement in capital markets.

In June 2018, I was appointed as Chairman of South Asian Federation of Exchanges (SAFE) for a period of one year. SAFE is a forum of 28 member entities from the SAARC region and neighbouring countries which aims to provide a platform to share, exchange and promote the technologies and experiences of capital markets coupled with regional as well as global integration.

On October 1, 2018, BSE launched commodity derivatives trading in Gold, Silver, Copper, Oman Crude Oil, Guar Gum and Seeds & Turmeric.

BSE provides a host of other services to capital market participants, including risk management, clearing, settlement, market data services and education. It has a global reach with customers around the world and a nation-wide presence.

As a step towards assisting capital markets by creating well informed investors, 'BSE Institute Ltd.' was revamped to facilitate knowledge sharing and now the enrolments for its courses are growing, a clear indication that newcomers are keen to have formal knowledge.

BSE will now act as a direct insurance broker under the IRDAI (Insurers Brokers) Regulations, 2018. BSE-Ebix Insurance Broking Pvt. Ltd., will enable distribution outlets, Wealth Management advisors, Point of Sales (POSs) to sell life and non-life insurance products.

BSE, along with PTC India Limited and ICICI Bank Limited, has asked for a license to set up a new Power Exchange.

Once active, it will facilitate funding of Power Projects and associated infrastructure, setting-up and running various exchanges and platforms in India, and offer the market participants a credible power trading platform.

I envision that BSE should become a Fintech company, venturing into new areas, by consolidating on its strengths and reputation, revamping itself and set higher benchmarks in performance.

The exchange man

THROUGH THE RINGMASTER'S LENS

BSE CEO Ashish Chauhan likens his job to a trapeze artist, assured by the excitement around. And there are times when punters are bowled by their own greed

14 PEOPLE WHO RUN MUMBAI

THE CITY'S INVISIBLE HEROES

MUMBAI MATTERS They have no names, they won't figure in history books, they are not famous. They are the invisible hands that move this city, and make our lives a little easier. Here's a glimpse into their lives.

ONLY MONEY MATTERS ON THIS STREET

BRINGING PAST ALIVE, ONE WALK AT A TIME

Boss of the Bourses

ASHISHKUMAR CHAUHAN, MD & CEO, BOMBAY STOCK EXCHANGE (BSE)

Little did Ashishkumar Chauhan know that he would witness a turnaround of BSE from a sluggish stock market to an agile platform. The man in question has been leading from the front for the last 10 years when he decided to join the 144-year-old institution. The IIT Mumbai and IIM Calcutta alumnus has a reputation of a leader who gets things done even in the most difficult circumstances. From IDBI Bank to National Stock Exchange of India to Reliance, Chauhan has always been at the helm of things. Talking about the risk he took while joining BSE, he says, "BSE was considered a declining brand when I joined. Now, it is considered as one of the best success stories which has regained some portion of its past glory."

Adapting to technology, according to Chauhan, was the toughest time in his decade-long journey. He shares, "It is like changing the heart of the person while he is running. He can't even stop to breathe. It has been remarkable how the BSE team achieved it almost in 10 per cent of the time it had taken another exchange and in a fraction of cost for capital expenditures as well as operating expenditure." In early 1990s and then later on in early 2000s, BSE faced several scandals. Even though other exchanges also had similar problems in 2000s, BSE was aggressively under scanner due to its past and lack of credible management. "I am delighted to say that today, BSE enjoys much better reputation for its compliances and fair business practices in India," claims Chauhan.

BSE also became the first exchange to list 300 companies and is the market leader with 60 per cent market share. The total amount of money raised through this platform is Rs 3,184 crore as of August 31, 2019. To augment its SME platform, BSE has enabled capital raising for start-ups via 'Startups' platform. Alphalogic Techsys and Transpact Enterprises are the first companies to get listed on the BSE Startups Platform on September 5, 2019.

A DAY IN THE LIFE OF ASHISH

"I start my day doing puja and conclude it again with puja and meditation. It is a very personal puja, which is a part of my family tradition. Before going to sleep, a few minutes of meditation clean up the mind and allow a good night's sleep. I have done a 10-day Vipassana meditation and Art of Living courses for a couple of times. I also try to learn newer meditation techniques whenever possible."

આશિષકુમાર ચૌહાણ

શેરબજારના સર્વેસર્વા...

મેકેનિકલ એન્જિનિયરિંગની ડિગ્રી અને પછી કોલકાતાની 'આઈઆઈએમ'માંથી એમબીએની પદવી લઈને એક યુવાન આઈડીબીઆઈ બેન્કમાં પ્રોજેક્ટ ફાઈનાન્સ ઓફિસર તરીકે જોડાય છે. જો કે એને કાંઈક એવું કરવું છે, જે ફાઈનાન્સિયલ વર્લ્ડમાં સીમાચિહ્નરૂપ ગણાય.

૧૯૯૩માં માત્ર પચીસ વર્ષની વયે આ યુવાન 'નેશનલ સ્ટોક એક્સચેન્જ' (એનએસઈ)ના સ્થાપકોમાંનો એક બને છે. આવનારા વર્ષોમાં આ એક્સચેન્જ એશિયાના સૌથી જૂના શેરબજાર અર્થાત્ 'બોમ્બે સ્ટોક એક્સચેન્જ' (બીએસઈ)ને ઝૂઝાવવાનું છે. આ યુવાન એટલે ગઈ કાલના ગુજરાતી આશિષકુમાર ચૌહાણ.

૧૯૯૪માં 'એનએસઈ'માં ડેરિવેટિવ્ઝ દાખલ કરીને એ 'ફ્યૂચર એન્ડ ડેરિવેટિવ્ઝ'નું વિશ્વ રચવી લે છે. એનએસઈ-૫૦ નામનો નવો સૂચકાંક હોય કે 'એનએસઈ' માટે સેટેલાઈટ આધારિત ટેલિકોમ નેટવર્કની ગોઠવણી હોય, તમામમાં એમના હાથ રહ્યા છે. આજે એનએસઈના જ પ્રતિસ્પર્ધી સેવા 'બીએસઈ'ના ઈન્ટરીમ સીઈઓ તરીકે કુરજ બજાવતા આશિષ ચૌહાણના કરિયરનો ગ્રાફ તો જે કે 'એનએસઈ છોડ્યા પછી પણ સતત ઊંચે જ ચઢતો રહ્યો છે અત્યારે એ 'બીએસઈ'ના હોદ્દ અને 'ઈન્ડિયન રિલાયન્સ કોર્પોરેશન્સ લિમિટેડ' (આઈઆરસીએલ)ના મેનેજિંગ ડિરેક્ટર ઉપરાંત બીજી કેટલીક કંપનીઓના ડિરેક્ટરપદ પણ શોભાવે છે.

૨૦૦૦ના નાળામાં 'એનએસઈ' છોડીને આશિષ નવ વર્ષ રિલાયન્સ જૂથના ગ્રૂપ ચીફ ઈન્ફોર્મેશન ઓફિસર (સીઆઈઓ) પદે રહ્યા.

હવે 'બીએસઈ'ના સભ્યો ડિલિવરી આધારિત ડેરિવેટિવ્ઝ, વેબ આધારિત આઈપીઓ, મ્યુચ્યુઅલ ફંડ વિતરણ જેવી અનેક સવલત ઊભી કરી છે.

બીએસઈની જવાબદારી સંભાળવા ઉપરાંત આશિષકુમાર ચૌહાણ 'સેન્ટ્રલ બોર્ડ ઓફ ડાયરેક્ટ ટેક્સિસ' (સીબીડીટી) તથા 'સેબી'ની કેટલીક કમિટી સાથે પણ સંકળાયેલા છે.

INDIA INX

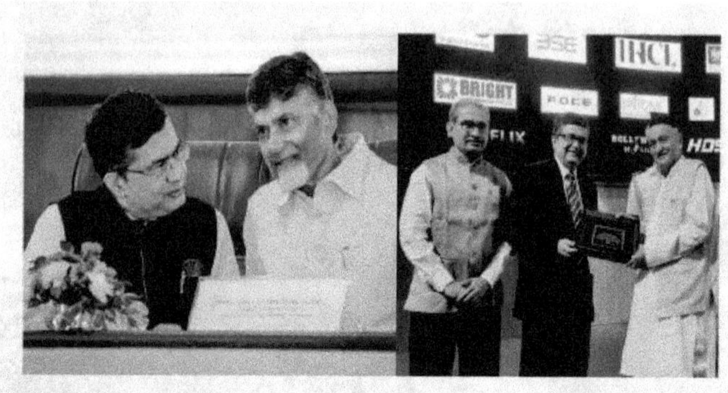

ASHISH CHAUHAN
JULIE MONACO
ROBERT DONNEL

CON MUMBAI 2019
Invest in India Summit 2015
Financing for Future Growth
12 January 2015
TABLE NO. 2

STHITAPRAGYA

Chapter 9

Technology *....the major change agent.*

'There is no wisdom for a man without harmony, and without harmony there is no contemplation. Without contemplation there cannot be peace, and without peace can there be joy?'

Bhagwad Geeta

I strongly believe that Technology is the only agent of change, a new way to do the same thing, done earlier. I am a great enthusiast and early adopter of Technology, and always think how the inexorable integration of technology in our lives could enhance some of our quintessential human capacities.

Technology is fascinating. It is the result of human efforts, applied in the right direction to help fellow human beings, the nation and the world. It's a speed facilitator and creates myriad avenues of development.

Let me give you an example, one of the first technologies discovered or invented in the world was how to control fire. Fire, existed even before mankind. However, it was untamed, and hence of very little use to man.

Whoever invented or discovered the ability to create fire on demand and control it within small spaces achieved substantial advantage, forever.

This technology of 'ability to control fire' slowly spread across the world.

Societies which adapted to the new technology had better longevity of life, had better food and could use fire as a weapon against other societies. They could even defend themselves from wild animals by lighting fire in the night. This technology took several thousand years to spread across the world. There are still societies which still worship fire. There were several other technologies invented at various times in the ancient era like the wheel, tools made by bones and so on.

Subsequent technologies like extracting metal from soil and making weapons from them, to be used in day to day life, have transformed the way we live.

Societies which came in contact with these technologies improved the quality of life for their members substantially, even when they could not master the technology themselves.

Post 'Renaissance' was the time frame within which new technologies got introduced and started accelerating.

Now, Science and technology became important. Steam Engine and subsequent technologies brought in the industrial revolution. Agrarian societies, which were stable for thousands of years, started breaking up.

People migrated to cities, abandoning their fields. Capitalism was born.

Society was changing rapidly with the advent of technology, but it still took a few generations. People didn't realize that changes in the society were happening due to technology.

During the early stages of Industrial Revolution the new elites began to appear, these were the businessmen. Aspirations increased. The French revolution took place. One after the other, many countries became democratic, to accommodate the aspirations of its people.

Soon, a new era was born in Europe that of acknowledging nobility by one's work and not defined by birth.

The moral of the story so far is that technology is the only change agent. Societies change in response to changing technology. Monarchies and Federal States became democratic in a span of 200 years. Central Banks got established. 'Nation States' were redefined. Law, Justice, Equality, everything we hold dear now are outcomes of these technological changes, not social!

At that time, technological changes were still slower, they would span generations. That is why a majority of people and societies could not comprehend the relativity between 'technological change' and 'social change'.

Off-late the technology waves have become faster. Earlier a technology change roughly took a thousand years, then it started taking in a couple of hundred years, then it shrunk to a few decades.

In the last 60 years, technology has spread over the entire world at a much faster pace. My generation has seen one single technology start, become mature and now spawns many more subsequent waves of technologies within the last 50-60 years.

Look at these facts:

Steam engine - discovered in the late 1600s took centuries to conceptualize, create and disseminate.

Electricity - discovered in the 1800s also took centuries to conceptualize, create and disseminate, but the span was shorter than the steam engine

Television - discovered in the 1920s, TVs went from concept to mass production over decades, and the technology is still evolving.

Mobiles - conceptualized in the 1970s, have taken fewer decades as compared to television

Google - started in 1998 took about 10 years, it completely altered the way we use the internet.

Facebook - started in 2007. In less than 10 years, it has become one of the biggest companies in the world

See how in a span of just one generation, information technology changed our lives completely, thoroughly, and radically.

Technology and technological changes should be welcomed with open arms.

Many a times it is harnessed to function and resolve some specific problem. But if we grasp its essence, it's in our control to experiment and use it in other areas, with a slight change of application, which makes it exciting. Once something is invented, it is available for the entire mankind, to intelligently adapt it for further development in diverse areas.

All developments in technology very soon become an integral part of our lives. You might have observed that whenever a new technology is introduced, it usually faces a lot of resistance. Once we begin to start seeing the results, we all welcome the change, so much so that it creates an aspiration for more, and we do say 'if this is possible, why we can't go a step further?'

This is the quest, a hunger that gives mankind a direction and I strongly believe that we are all invariably being driven by technology.

For me the advent of Technology signified 'possibilities galore'. The application of any technology in new areas, in order to provide a solution, gave me the energy to keep striving. A problem is seen as a problem, because we tend to see it only from a single perspective, which is the conventional approach of following age old practices. Change the perspective by questioning "why not?" and you get the answer and the solution. That 'why not' is the key to create an agent of change.

Many a times, during the process of applying technology in a new domain, we tend to give up with a sense of failure, because it's not an easy task. It needs persistence, continuous efforts and detailed logical approach. And it was this spirit which I inculcated in all the teams I worked with, which led us all to achieve great landmarks, some of which changed the destiny of the entire country. 'Yes, we can do it' that resounding unanimous affirmation, is such a heartening victory call!

Post schooling, fate decided to surprise me with new responsibilities, but rather than being apprehensive, I always saw an opportunity in every challenge. All I did was to apply logic and put in sincere efforts to better the working. This commitment and passion resulted in me enjoying adventures of different kinds, each thrilling, sometimes scary, but always satisfying.

A brief look at some important milestones created, thanks to technology and its adept application.

Automated Screen Based Trading.
The advent of screen based trading, the first time in India for NSE, changed the history of Indian Stock Markets forever. It also was one of the first few successful experiments of automation of 'trading' in the world. Post NSE's success, other global exchanges like NYSE, London Stock Exchange, NASDAQ became screen based. This success was a path breaker in a way. It became a showcase of confidence for the Indian technology fraternity, that we were better than the best in the world.

First Private 'Two way' Satellite Telecommunication.
This was a gigantic and revolutionary step that connected all Indian Stock Markets. Earlier there were several exchanges, each working on single platforms, at a time when a single nationwide order book was unheard of.

The use of Satellites for Communication, despite huge opposition from giants like BSNL, ISRO and other authorities, gave birth to a modern hi tech India.

This technology also enabled most of the banks to start providing ATMs. Connected to a satellite, they could manage their central databases easily to offer services to people.

B2B E Commerce

My venture, 'exchangenext.com' was an interesting experiment. Almost all marketplaces set up in 1999-2001 didn't move forward, due to lack of internet speed and other issues. However, this initiative was one of the predecessors of the much larger B2B and B2C companies that were set up later on.

Mobile Telephony

I was part of the team that brought affordable mobile connectivity to every Indian, by bringing down the price from ₹ 16 per minute to 20 paise per minute. This huge reduction in billing, in just one week, brought millions of new users and a decade later, India had more than a billion telephone connections. From 1947 to 2004, India had 40 Million land line connections. From 2004 to 2014, India added 1000 Million mobile connections.

Organised Retail

I was in charge of the team that provided automation technology to India's largest chain of retail stores, which operate from grocery to electronics to jewellery, in all formats from super markets, departmental stores, stand alone speciality stores to multi retail. Today this technology is working wonderfully and is making life so convenient for people all over the country.

Modernised Petrochemicals and Refining

I was involved in modernizing the technology for old plants and transforming them into hi tech plants in Petrochemicals and Refining. These are amongst the largest plants India has seen till date.

Deep sea drilling for Oil and Gas exploration

I was involved in providing latest technology to some of the most innovative deep sea drilling activities, in perpetual rough seas, at a depth we in India had never explored before.

Automation of Nationwide Gas pipelines

I was involved in providing state-of- the- art technology for automation and commercial platforms to one of the largest pipelines in India.

Stock Markets

I have been lucky to have worked in some of the most important and exciting projects in Stock Markets post 1991, and played a pivotal role in many internet based trading in markets.

We managed to enable internet and CTC trading, while working for NSE. It opened up the market, which was earlier meant for traders with high cost leased lines, to small investors. It democratized Indian markets and allowed many more people to trade from the nooks and corners of India.

Derivatives

The introduction of derivatives was one of the most defining achievements of my career. It needed a lot of effort, from ideation to marketing to writing regulations, preparing technology, implementing the risk management framework, creation of Nifty index, getting laws amended etc. I had to answer many committees on the subject, teach the concepts at colleges, and speak at more than 500 forums over 5 years, to make people aware of this concept and its process.

I have been called the 'Father of Indian financial Derivatives Market' since the year 2000. This was because from 1995 to 2000, I worked ceaselessly to conceptualise and position trading of derivatives in Indian financial markets.

Creation of Nifty Index

The NIFTY index was created with my colleagues at NSE and external help was provided by Dr Ajay Shah and Dr Susan Thomas of IGIDR. Nifty has now become the most traded Indian index. A strategic tie up with 'Standard and Poor' and housing it in a separate company called 'India Index Services Private Limited' was also achieved successfully.

Public Relations for the largest business house of India

I acted as the Head of Public Relations for Reliance Group for several years. It was tougher compared to handling IT for a USD 100 billion Group.

Running of IPL Cricket team

I was lucky to also be the CEO of IPL cricket team 'Mumbai Indians' in its formative years. It being the first season, not many people knew how to organize so many matches in the same city, in quick succession and provide for the logistics like ticket sales, merchandising, security, on ground advertisements, sponsorships, facilities management, and complete customer management. In addition it also entailed managing cricket stadiums, lights, kits, masseurs, physiotherapists for super star cricketers and super star spectators, as also providing facilities to the competing team and making them feel welcome, with changing stadium locales and cities.

The second season saw me facing even tougher challenges as the IPL matches were to be played in South Africa, across seven cities, on a short notice of less than a month.

Initial business plan and work for India's first depository - NSDL
Initial technology conceptualisation and also interior decoration of NSDL offices were done in less than teo months, to make it ready for inauguration, complete with a Data Centre. This task was full of hardships.

Large successful IPO's - pre and post listing
I have been involved in planning and execution of some of the most interesting IPO's that of BSE and Reliance Petroleum, with some of the largest oversubscriptions. In both issues, pre issue negativity was quite high, but the over subscriptions and post issue performance were amazing.

For the BSE issue, getting the permissions and go ahead after 10 years of continuous efforts by itself was a great achievement. Then came the challenge of pulling it off, in spite of very little or no support from existing numerous shareholders. This achievement was not short of a miracle, with an oversubscription over 51 times.

BSE

At BSE, technology swept away the dust and reputation of a 'fossiled' stock exchange. Today it has achieved a world record of 6 micro seconds of response time! At BSE we have developed many innovative products like Incubator, SME, Mutual Fund Distribution, Insurance distribution, Currency market leadership, Bond distribution, Power Exchange etc.

Mobile Trading

We conceived a radical idea and then, with persistent efforts, got the Mobile Trading in Indian Stock Markets, launched at par with best in the world. We won with this innovation, in spite of the opposition and obfuscation, from all those who wanted to prove that they had a regulatory control.

The India International Exchange 'India INX'

The Hon'ble CM of Gujarat in 2013 and now the Hon'ble PM of India, Shri Narendra Modi invited us to help set up a 'state of the art' International Exchange in Gandhinagar Gift City. BSE signed up to set up the Exchange during Vibrant Gujarat in 2015 and on Jan 9, 2017, the Hon'ble PM inaugurated it.

This Exchange provides trading to foreigners and competes with Dubai, Singapore, Hong Kong and London. It trades only in dollars and other currencies, not in Indian rupees. For all practical purposes, it is a foreign territory.

In just a year, India INX was doing business of over USD 0.4 Billion per day Many more activities are yet to be allowed there. The progress made in one year has been stupendous.

So much was done in just two decades. Now technology is advancing still faster, in leaps of five to ten years. I anticipate the structural changes in society to be massive.

I feel strongly that India has got a chance to bounce back after almost 500 years of being complacent. It has the potential of becoming the richest country in the world in coming 40 years. In the years to follow, we will create wealth that has not been created in 10,000 years, by using new technology. We would also create over 70% jobs that we cannot even visualise now!

We have already entered into a non linear phase, as far as wealth creation is concerned. Conventionally 'wealth created wealth', was the basic principle of capitalism. But now you can invest one rupee and become a millionaire, or invest nothing at all to become one. That's because technology has given us this greatest boon to set up new profit making avenues.

The world's largest taxi firm Uber, doesn't own a single car, and the world's largest media company, Facebook, creates no content, and then there is the world's largest accommodation provider AIRBNB, which doesn't own a single property! It is sheer application of technology and ingenuity!

A game like 'Pokemon Go' amassed 50 million users in 19 days, which took automobile users 62 years to achieve, telephone users 50 years and credit card users 28 years!

If Information Technology changed lives, there are many more technologies that are coming which will transform life completely.

Robotics: Robots are expanding skills, showing awesome productivity and retention rates, and increasingly replacing their human counterparts. One multi-tasker robot, can make (and flip) a gourmet burger in 10 seconds and could soon replace an entire McDonalds crew

Virtual Reality: The next evolution of VR would be where you participate physically in that VR world. And not just sitting down; like in cricket, if you're a fast bowler, you actually get to bowl, and you can interface with the team. So that kind of stuff, it's there, it's going to happen.

Artificial Intelligence: Automation could transform the way we work by replacing humans with machines and software. One step further, Artificial intelligence (AI) is software built to learn or 'problem solve' processes typically performed by the human brain.

Drones: When filmmaker George Lucas popularized 'droids' — worker robots designed to tend to humanity's every need — in the 1977 movie 'Star Wars: Episode IV - A New Hope,' he seemed like a sci-fi visionary. But today, it has become main stream. In the future, drones are guaranteed to have application in varied industries ranging from logistics, travel to agriculture and regular photography.

Space Technology: Rapid advances in space technologies will one day take us to asteroids, Mars and back to the Moon, and the impact of these missions will be felt back on Earth. These innovations are also used in almost every facet of society, from our phone and furniture to aviation and healthcare. Space technologies are likely to solve some of humanity's biggest challenges

Gene-editing technology allows DNA to be edited easily, raising hopes that it could eventually be used to relieve human suffering and ultimately redefine human life. Would you want to alter your future children's genes to make them smarter, stronger or better-looking? As the state of the science brings prospects like these closer to reality, we are on the brink of a brave new world of genetically enhanced humanity

Wearable computing: Wearable technology is simply a 'transition' technology. Technology must and will soon move from existing outside our bodies to residing inside us. The next big frontier is 'Implantable wearable's.

Ubiquitous Mobile supercomputing, 3-D Printing, Nano Technology, Inside Body Wearable Computing, Internet of Things, Big Data, Self driven cars, Neuro technological Brain Enhancements will enhance human life over the next three decades.

Very soon we will be spending more and more time in the virtual world and augmented reality. We are standing at the threshold of a technological revolution that will fundamentally alter the way we live, work and relate to one another. In its scale, scope and complexity, this transformation will be unlike anything humankind has ever experienced before!

And the evidence of technological prowess is all around us, happening at an exponential speed. If we build and foster an optimistic attitude at this point of time, it will help enhance productivity and solve innumerable problems, ranging from healthcare to transportation.

Technology is like a fluid. Adapt it, guide it, give it the flow in right direction and it creates personal, social and national wealth.

STHITAPRAGYA

Chapter 10

Interdisciplinary facets ..... *religion, philosophy and society*

'We are not cabin-dwellers, born to a life cramped and confined. We are meant to explore, to seek, to push the limits of our potential as human beings. The world of the senses is just a base camp, we are meant to be as much at home in consciousness as in the world of physical reality.'

Bhagwad Geeta

I was nurtured in a home which was full of devotional fervour and this has had a very calming effect on me. It awakened an unusual curiosity to understand the meaning of rituals, religion and beliefs. And perhaps on a broader scale, understand our relationships with fellow beings. My grandmother would practice a set of rituals as well as take me along for discourses of Dongre Maharaj, Murari

Bapu, etc. Listening to discourses of the learned, recitals of scriptures and discussions at home plus reading a lot of literature were fanning many aspects of spiritualism at my tender age.

Because certain terminologies of 'adhyatma' or spiritualism were beyond my comprehension at such an early age, I would read a lot of religious literature like the Bhagwad Geeta, Quran, Bible etc. All of these were available in Gujarati and were written for children. Even magazines like 'Jana Kalyan', 'Akhand Anand', had informative articles. A young boy taking keen interest in such literature, convinced most of my family members that I would eventually become a monk!

But I was interested in religious philosophies not purely as religion but as an integral part of social and economic thoughts. I had read up numerous books, scriptures and their interpretations as to how societies get together, learn to stay together and work productively together. In absence of any framework, societies find it difficult to survive. Equality of all citizens is a modern thought, but finds an echo in many old scriptures. It was also obvious that most scriptures and religious texts across religions had their own odd unusual and unbelievable stories, mirroring the context of the times and societies in which they evolved. Some of them focused more on society and some on individuals.

After reading a lot for almost 5 decades, added to the life experiences I had, I have come to the conclusion that, as compared to a 'no order - no authority' situation, some type of order and authority is better than anarchy for survival of the society and the poorest among them.

Anarchy is more harmful to the people at the lower level, as compared to any other order. Within that framework, everyone has to try to achieve equality. Democracies with 'majoritarian' streak are much better than 'authoritarian' states, in achieving better equality. But Democracies do it slowly and so they may not be able to achieve a faster growth, as compared to authoritarian states.

I had also been interested in Buddhism and its philosophy of 'No God' and concepts of 'karma', 'reincarnation', 'eight fold paths' etc.

Reading books on Marxism and Lenin, made available in Gujarati, opened up new vistas of understanding religious philosophies in a social context.

Generally, the middle class Indians in 70's and late 80's had a dislike for an over ritualistic life, which is true even today. But I had no inhibition of belonging to a religiously inclined family. In fact, it gave me the opportunity to talk to monks and sages. Being a vernacular medium student was also a great advantage, as it helped me understand religion and philosophy, in my mother tongue.

Hindu religion and philosophy emphasises on finding oneself – 'Where I come from', 'Who am I'. Self search is the essence of its texture. Hinduism has a hierarchical approach.

Islamic religion, theoretically, treats everyone as equal.

Born as a new path towards realisation and moving away from the 'over ritualistic' Hindu practices, Buddhism and Jainism propagated curtailment of desires and penance.

Both these completely changed the concept of God, as seen from the Hindu perspective.

After I learnt English, I read about non-indic philosophies like those of Kant and Confucius etc. This keen interest also inspired me to take up Philosophy as an elective subject in college, which offered short courses on meditation and other subjects. Both IIT and IIM had excellent teachers. Thanks to such opportunities, I gained valuable insights of religion and philosophy and could comprehend them, scaling boundaries of a limited and structured thinking.

Studying Western philosophy gave me the understanding that they have always made a clear distinction between Religion and Society. Both these were treated distinctly. This was in sharp contrast to Indian philosophy which used to interconnect them.

Socrates and Plato had contributed a lot to the concept of a modern Nation and State.

This distinction happened because of the way Europe evolved. Democracy helped them in demarcating State and Religion and so over 500 years they have evolved faster than us in India.

As per western belief, each individual has to be given a right to pursue his or her own happiness. Whereas in Indian society, the emphasis is more on collective thinking, propagating that an individual is just a part of a larger scheme of things. This means that an individual does not have his or her rights, but is bound by society and hierarchy.

As I delved deeper into this subject I discerned that religion, ethics, morality, were all existing in a 'time - space' framework, controlled by changes that were taking place in society. The tone of the philosophy, within the religion, is always set during that 'timeframe' and it is deeply embedded in the warp and weft of the society. Society functions as a living thing. It is continuously evolving. And as it evolves, it adapts to new norms and sets new behavioural patterns, which become the guidelines for the next generation.

I believe that religion was always more relevant in the context of society, set in a specific period. Take for example the society during Bhagwan Krishna's time, Bhagwan Ram's time or Bhagwan Buddha's time, each was in a different time and space. The society during 'Ramayan' times was less complex but later during 'Mahabharata', it became more complex, because it had evolved. In this process some past learning's were retained, the rest became irrelevant and were discarded. That which was considered good in a certain timeframe may not be considered good in another and strangely, in some cases, what was considered good about 5000 years ago, is still relevant today.

There is an interesting mythological story. Krishna and Arjun while playing had burnt an entire jungle and the birds had cursed them that the way they burnt their families, living in the trees, the Yadav and Pandu community would be destroyed at one stroke, and this actually happened. Now look at it from a social context. Their burning of a jungle was not a game perhaps, it was their need to acquire more land and extend their kingdom, a step towards further evolvement. In the scripture it has been presented as a story.

Religion was meant to make an individual lead a more meaningful life, but there was also a social aspect in every phase, each with its particular texture. As society evolved, it created new laws, which become part of religion. I deduce that religion and philosophy play a small part in connecting us to a higher power or God. The major role of religion is in the social context, focused on an individual's behaviour with other human beings.

Some religion has 'one' God, some 'no' God and some 'many' Gods. At the core of this framework, we are being taught how to function in a more orderly manner in a society, and 'order' is contextual. So it doesn't necessarily mean one order is good and the other is bad.

Within a society, groups of individuals created sects, based on a certain philosophy. In each sect one noticed some sort of regimentation, for instance in the Swami Narayan sect, we are told not to eat garlic or onion, not to see movies and not to take intoxicants. The Swadhayay sect, which follows the principles of Shri Pandurang Athavle, has its own norms on principles that Pandurangji followed. You can clearly see the regiment aspect of any sect, which are guidelines created to mould you and your behaviour with family members and society.

There are so many sects that exist in our country, some organised and some unorganised. Take for instance BAPS. It was a very small movement, not even a sect, about 60 years ago. As they progressed over the years, they made themselves relevant to the changing society in Gujarat, by becoming more organised and inclusive. Today we can see their astonishing growth trajectory which has got a phenomenal following. Then there are unorganised sects like the Shirdi Sai Baba. It has no regimentation and yet it has grown in enormous numbers. This is also true with the 'Deras' in the north and 'Matths' in the south.

2000 years ago, India was more advanced than other societies in the world. Even in 1650, India's GDP was 25% of the worlds GDP. Then Europe embarked on its journey of Industrial Revolution. Ironically they used many of our ideas to flourish! By 1950, when the British left, India's GDP became 2% of world GDP! Imagine how much wealth was created in those 300 years, which got transferred to the West!

The subjugation by the western countries antiquated us. We, in India invented the zero, but didn't much use it. We also invented Plastic Surgery, Maths and Science but did not use it to improve the society and achieve material progress. We did not evolve in defence and armaments. All our innovations were used by the western countries to their advantage, helping their growth and prosperity.

One good thing was that the British rule ended up changing a lot of our fabric of religion and social norms. The Hindu religion, pre British era, had a rigid caste system and ritualistic practices like Sati etc, which got abolished. After almost 1000 years of anachronism, an external jolt given by them, initiated a faster reform for our society.

The lessons to be learnt are that we have to be less hierarchical and more equal amongst our brethren to advance. We must learn to tolerate each other and maintain coherence to protect ourselves from outside forces.

As we look into the future, it is exciting to know how societies will change, of course this will be very very fast now, thanks to technology and virtual reality. Isn't it a fact that a few decades ago we lived in a neighbourhood, set in geographical boundaries, but now because of mobiles and virtual reality, though we are physically present at a location, our minds are away, where we think we have found likeminded people. Even on the dining table, each member of the family is using his/her phone, and not present in mind, though physically present! Soon, we all may become like islands! Living together, but not connected at all. Will it not completely change the texture of society and its norms? It is not good or bad, that's how it will be.

When India became Independent, life expectancy averaged at 39 years, is now around 69 years, and with help of advanced medicine, the further we go into the future, life expectancy may be averaging at 150 years! If this happens what happens to the population? All the norms of society will change and even at the age of 100 we would be called young!

The evolution of a totally new society will change so many parameters of living and behaviour towards each other! Our current laws may become increasingly irrelevant as laws are created based on collective past experiences. The future is advancing rapidly and is beyond our control. It is almost like driving a car looking only at the rear-view mirror. Future laws will have to be anticipated. Past experiences of the society will not be a good guide to the future.

Societies ready to adopt their laws and way of life, taking advantage of new incoming technologies, will survive and thrive. Those who do not have a flexible framework may find themselves at a disadvantage. The set order in the society, like the elites and non elites, and hierarchies may also change rapidly.

At present, the individual as a body is one unit and finite, but if a virtual brain on the internet, takes control and helps us transfer all our experiences, our memories and mistakes, on a day to day basis, perhaps in decades to come even after physical death we might remain alive, either individually or collectively, in some combination!

A silent chaos is coming at a fast speed, like a tsunami. Fighting and trying to sail upstream is not a choice. Sailing with the tsunami is the only choice. Of course the ride will be uncomfortable for societies and its people. But if anyone will try to jump out of it, he or she will be drowned.

The intertwining of religion, philosophy and society is an interesting observation, and it is entirely our choice to seek a path of self development which also gives us inner peace.

STHITAPRAGYA

Chapter 11

Ménage ......*my family*

'Seek refuge in the attitude of detachment and you will amass the wealth of spiritual awareness. Those who are motivated only by desire for the fruits of action are miserable, for they are constantly anxious about the results of what they do.'

Bhagwad Geeta

I have been fortunate that I was brought up in a family practicing the virtues of truth, sincerity and acceptance.

My grandmother was my darling. Looking at her I would be inspired to be as loving and doting as she was. And even as she aged, her resolve to be independent was with sheer will power. She lived in a very dignified manner. She was the first to have introduced me to the world of philosophy, that which has been the backbone of my attitude in life – 'Sthitapragya.'

Then of course are my parents. My father always supported me in my education and inculcated the values of righteousness while performing duties, without succumbing to any pressure. He always worked for the betterment of society, being least bothered about personal comforts or status.

As for my mother, her dedication to education which gave her an opportunity to take up a job was a big support, not only to the immediate family, but the extended family too. Her ability to multi task was amazing, everything done with ease and absolutely no complaints. An ideal mother, truly endowed with the power of 'Shakti' and benevolence, she has had the maximum influence on me, and is my role model.

My mother had come from a fairly affluent family. After her father's sudden demise, she had to earn to pay for her fees, and unlike many women, she wanted to pursue her education. Fortunately her skill of intricate and exclusive embroidery, made her capable of earning enough to study.

She won the coveted Gold Medal in Economics, under the guidance of Shri Chimanbhai Patel, former CM of Gujarat. At that time he was teaching in a college in Gujarat, before joining politics.

She had met my father in college. As her brother and my father were close friends, my father used to go to her house often and soon they decided to get married. Having stayed in a city throughout, after marriage when my mother shifted to our village, she managed to adapt herself to a different lifestyle, which must have been tough. Thankfully, later they did shift back to Ahmedabad again.

Her passion for embroidery continued till her old age, as a hobby, as she liked the intricate work of hands.

When my sister Beena was expecting her child, she called my mother to the US, and my mother was more than happy to go and take care of her grandchild. After her first visit, she continued to go off and on. At times my father and she alternated their visits.

In late 90's, my mother was at my sister's house in the US. At bedtime, she suddenly developed chest pain. My sister rushed her to the hospital, but before reaching there, she had left for her heavenly abode.

At that time I was attending my second 'Vipasana' camp at Igatpuri, except my secretary, no one knew where I was.

Half way in to the course, in the middle of a night, the office of the Vipasana foundation called me to meet them. I was told that my mother was serious and I needed to contact my family in US. I contacted them and they informed me that she had expired due to a massive heart attack at my sister's house.

I took a vehicle to Mumbai from Igatpuri and went to my apartment, woke up my younger brother and told him that mother had expired in US and that both of us were to go to Ahmedabad. We took the first flight, at 5 am. My father was hospitalized on listening about my mother's demise and we had to take care of him too.

It was a very stressful period personally, career wise, health wise and overall. My personal disposition to take things in stride and practice of Vipasana helped me go through the trauma to some extent. That period changed my personal perspective and life quite a lot. I was quite careless and took my immediate family for granted earlier. Though my focus on work and career still remained, the stress of job came down to zero. I decided not to work in pursuit of position or money in future.

My brother, Sunil is tall. Even at the age of 12, he looked like an adult. He got involved in the manufacturing of computers and selling them at an early age. Academics were not his forte. When he was 17, he migrated to the US. Initially he took up some odd sales jobs, later worked at a grocery store and much later he opened his '7 to 11' store and other businesses.

My sister, Beena, is my second mother! Since the time I was a toddler, she used to shower so much care and attention, that I became completely dependent on her!

She was average in academics, and on completing her education had got a job in a bank. She was the one who bought the first vehicle in our household, a two wheeler.

In 1986, when I was at IIT, I got a message that my sister was getting married to a boy from the US. This was a sudden and surprising news for me, so I rushed to Ahmedabad and asked her, whether she wanted to migrate.

She said yes and so we all began to prepare for her marriage, which took place within a week. After six months of her marriage, she shifted to the US. Having studied in Gujarati medium like me, she did have a tough time with English. She took up a job in HR. Her husband, Mahesh Chudasama worked as a chemist, and had been in US for many years, prior to his marriage with Beena.

Beena has been a sheet anchor in every aspect of my life, since my childhood. Many family members still think my sister runs my life. She continues to pamper me even though I have crossed the age of 50! She extends extreme care and attention to every detail. I hardly buy any personal belongings, it is she who does that for me. I am fortunate that my wife doesn't have any issue with this.

Marriage for me happened all of a sudden. I had kept delaying it, but once I met Sonal, as per hindu arranged marriage tradition, we seemed to be made for each other.

I got engaged to Sonal and within a short period I got married to her, although she had to study for masters for some more time in Ahmedabad. We had a long distance marriage where she was in Ahmedabad and I was in Mumbai for some time. Her family was staying in interiors of Gujarat. In some ways, she was an antidote to many of my vices.

Till the age of 17, I did not even eat onions and garlic and was a strict vegetarian. It was during IIT days, I had started eating non vegetarian food, consuming alcohol, smoking cigarettes and chewing 'Gutkha' tobacco. It continued till our engagement, despite going through Vipasana and other meditation techniques.

While agreeing to marry me, Sonal put a condition that I will have to leave non vegetarian food, alcohol, cigarettes and chewing tobacco. It was a mix of religious and personal reasons for her.

For me, it was very difficult to agree. After a few initial hiccups, I have been able to fulfil my promises to her and quit non vegetarian food, alcohol and tobacco completely.

In retrospect, this decision was very helpful in managing my health condition of diabetes effectively. The implementation with no exception, made me more determined and disciplined. My long standing minor health issue of continual sore throat also disappeared. Earlier, I used to have sore throat every 15 days and had to take antibiotics frequently, which began to lose effect due to regular consumption. Leaving habits like chewing 'Gutkha' perhaps helped in removing sore throat permanently.

Sonal is a radiologist, she had started working with JJ Hospital, Mumbai once she completed her studies. My son, Shawn, was born in 2001. Between the years 2000 and 2010, we changed almost five houses, and that burden was all borne by my wife.

When my son was very young, he developed asthma, as we were living in Lower Parel, a developing area, where construction work was rampant. At that time I was terribly occupied with Reliance Infocom, and my office was in New Bombay, a far away distance. I used to reach home at wee hours, take my son to the hospital, come back by 7.30 am, get ready and leave for office again.

I had hardly any time to spare at home, but Sonal managed. Right through Shawn's toddler years to his teenage, she has taken care of his needs and given him the right upbringing.

Though Sonal is just 2 years younger to me, she looks twenty to thirty years younger. People find it hard to believe that we are married, looking so different in terms of age. She doesn't put in any efforts at looking young, but continues to look the same for last 20 years!

For children, Santa Claus is a mythical character who fulfils their wishes. For my son, it is his aunt Beena and uncle Sunil who pamper him to the hilt. He learnt very early how to make their hearts melt and get them to fulfil his demands.

As for me, as by now you all know my keen interests are cricket, reading and work. When I am relaxed, I can sit for hours without conversing. Ghazals, Hindi film music and reading are my favourite companions. Singers like Jagjit Singh. Mehndi Hassan, Ghulam Ali, Mukesh, Mohammad Rafi, Kishore Kumar, Manna Dey, Talat Aziz, Begum Akhtar, Ahmed Hussain, Mohammad Hussein are some of my favourites. Bhajans by Anup Jalota, Hari Om Sharan, Hemant Chauhan are calming. I also adore Abida Parvin, Rahat Fateh Ali khan and Arijit Singh!

While A R Rahman clearly has been a winner as a composer in the new generation, compositions of S D Burman, Kalyanji Anandji, Hemant Kumar are my favourites.

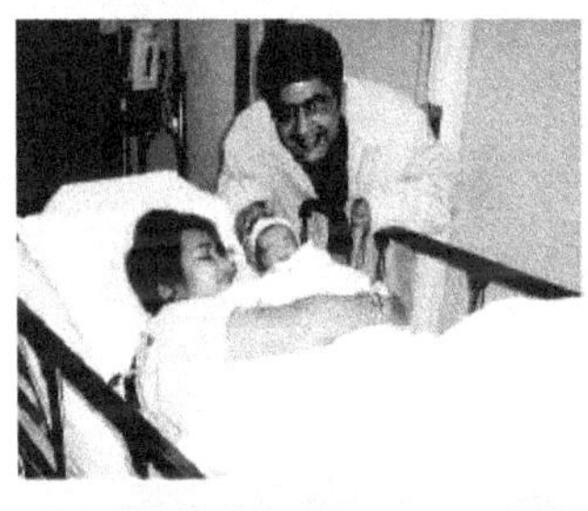
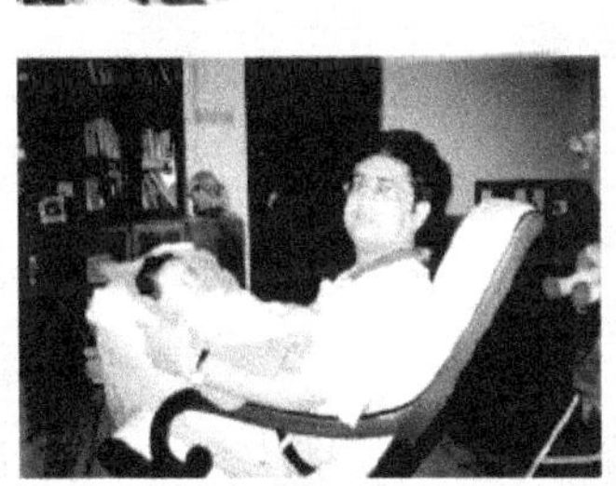
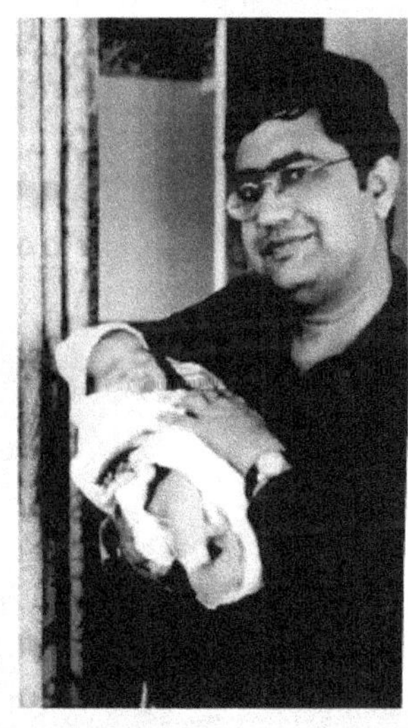

STHITAPRAGYA

Chapter 12

Jeevan Tatparya .....*life's purpose*

'You have the right to work, but never to the fruit of work. You should never engage in action for the sake of reward, nor should you long for inaction. Perform work in this world, Arjuna, as a man established within himself - without selfish attachments, and alike in success and defeat.'

Bhagwad Geeta

I have lived 10 lives in one lifespan. The fact that I was not born with a silver spoon, made me work hard for sheer survival. This became a boon for me, as I got enriched with varied experiences, each almost like a lifespan.

With a stoic resolve, faith in myself, astute principles and tremendous hard work, I consider being fortunate to have contributed my best to the organisations I worked for, who in turn contributed towards building a robust economy for the nation.

I believe that no matter what our circumstances, be it economic conditions, education, family or culture, it is entirely in our hands to maximise our potential and keep evolving. If we sit back and lament on what we don't have, or compare ourselves to others and feel limited, we do not gain anything except sorrow. But if we say 'I am happy with what I have, and will make every effort to learn more, work harder and be detached from selfish motives', the doors and windows of opportunities begin to open up.

It is tempting to day dream that life would have been easier if this or that was made available to me, but I looked at it from a different perspective. Whatever was available was the best I had been given and I had to make better of it!

I thank the Almighty that I was born in times where I could learn to apply my skills in various fields and they became game changers for the benefit of fellow human beings of my country.

The journey from a small village to BSE has been effervescent. I kept on following a gut instinct, with some amount of fearlessness and a great amount of self learning. Education and values were the only backing I had. I am glad that my simple upbringing and rock solid values prevented me from getting entrapped into any sort of greed to make quick money.

Post schooling, being alienated from my comfort zone was like being thrown into an ocean. In such a situation, we can either get overwhelmed by the water around us and drown or learn to swim. If we learn to swim, then the ocean becomes symbolic of limitless possibilities

Life is never a bed of roses. There were many blind curves and pitfalls I faced,

But each became an opportunity for me to overcome some limitations that I had. By accepting and overcoming my limitations, I became stronger.

It was my childlike enthusiasm that got me engrossed in work passionately. Work gave me countless opportunities that developed more and more skill sets.

Whatever came my way, I gave it more than 100%. Finding any shortcuts or shirking responsibility, either as an employee or a leader, a son, a husband, or a relative, is not in my nature. I try to do justice to all my responsibilities. I also consciously chose not be part of any influential group. Though this decision has hurt me badly in some instances, in the long run it gave me freedom to follow my own principles.

A major part of my life has been without any monies and zero ability to take risks. Despite that, I didn't hesitate in taking calculated risks. With a 16 hour day at work, with no weekend for leisure for the last 29 years, I know that the balance between leisure and work has been very uneven. But since my work is as comforting as leisure, I have never felt deprived of it.

I never envied the rich and famous and remained the same 'happy go lucky' ambitionless boy next door, wanting nothing from life except to live graciously.

The inner mental strength to multi task, to be able to concentrate on work, despite personal problems, was inculcated by observing my mother's life.

For being in a detached state, I would give credit to Vipasana meditation, which taught me to 'let go'. It was life changing and transformational. It has been the single factor responsible to keep me calm and remove any thoughts of personal benefit or personal comforts and always to take a broad approach in a more rational way.

As an individual, if I have to summarize the principles of good living, they would be:

Remain frugal - our basic needs are few. Once we give wings to aspirations and desires, more than we need, we lose the values of simple living.

Work with great passion - let there be zeal in your actions, driven by the thought that the work you do will benefit people, the organisation and eventually the country.

Believe - that the smallest action you take in the right direction will somehow help and lead society in the right direction. Don't restrict yourself by thinking that your action will not be counted among the millions.

Observe - the changes around and keep on evolving.

Mingle, interact and meet people - be socially active and be as useful as possible, to others.

Be compassionate - there are thousands who survive on a single meal or are roofless. Understand the problems of the poorest and do whatever you can to solve them.

Be forgiving - as human beings we are all equal, even if someone has been bad to you, due to his/her circumstances, don't be inimical. Forgive and wish good, don't nurture hatred.

Be gracious - try to help as many people as possible. It can be a smile, a word of encouragement, donation of monies or just a moral support.

Be humble - never let arrogance become your attitude, and never try to show off to others to make yourself feel better or more worthy.

Be selfless - keep yourself away from desires of personal gains. Greed never pays in the long run.

Let go - don't cling on to things or situations or even people. Always keep a large heart and learn to lose graciously.

Sleep well - sleep is important it calms the whole body and mind.

Be meditative - silence and meditation gives you better focus, clears the clutter in your mind, so meditate as much as you can.

Be supportive - observe and support people who wish to do some good for the society, they need help with more like minded people joining them in what they are trying to achieve.

And as an individual in an Organisation, I believe we must:

Be adaptive - the entire world is in a constant motion of change, so accept change graciously. Don't hold on to set patterns and norms. Change is good and healthy.

Be honest - always make yourself a trustee of others' or public money. Treat every rupee with respect. Utilise and channelize their monies in a better way than your own money.

Be human to colleagues - always connect to people on a human level. This helps in developing a good team. If we trust people they will perform with responsibility and feel proud about it.

Set high standards - as you begin to work, don't let yourself be mediocre. Work towards achieving a larger scale. If you attempt, you will succeed.

Be compliant - always adhere to compliance parameters of all regulations, no shortcut ever works. If rules have been laid down or principles have been formed, it is with a good thought, so be within that framework.

Plan our day - make your day to day management most efficient and give respect to the team. Give each team member the authority to take independent decisions and support their efforts.

Set an example - if you want to make a team work, then you must work harder than anyone in the team. Lead by actions and not words. Just by observing that you are working hard, inspires your team to join you with equal zest.

Be visionary - every action takes time to bring results at a macro level, so take long term bets.

Climb higher and higher - never become complacent and content with achievements. The moment you reach one benchmark, set another which is higher. If you have reached one, you will also reach the next level.

Be fearless - do not fear to experiment, let the work sphere become a laboratory where you try new methods and new formulas. Keep on testing, keep on trying as failures lead to success and give breakthroughs that lead to giant leaps.

Be non linear - if you take a path, see that you go for non linear pay off. This makes your actions multidimensional and gives multiple results.

Be righteous - never venture into a business or be a part of any activity that can hurt people, even if it is in an indirect manner.

Begin with small steps - small steps help build the momentum to scale up faster.

Don't be overconfident - sometimes overconfidence tricks us into situations that can be harmful to us. Always be alert of risks and be equally alert to see new opportunities.

Believe in team values - we must inculcate the spirit that we are working together as a team. Respect all authorities and abide by their decisions.

Be principled - take decisions and actions in tandem with the belief systems and principles of the government of the day.

Be calm when taking decisions - it is natural to get angry at times, but never take any decisions in moments of anger.

Be a mediator - when we are working with a large number of people, there is bound to be some friction. Try to solve or reduce friction, by being able to balance opposing views.

I believe that we must remain sensitive to every situation, at every stage of our lives. This helps in remaining responsible and accountable in performing our duties. When you take up responsibilities of a larger scale then your accountability becomes directly proportional to your responsibilities. And as you manoeuvre through the charted path, you realise that realities differ radically from theories, so you have to take a practical approach and arrive at suitable decisions, and mind you, each situation is different. There is no set formula.

In public life, the higher you climb the higher your restraints become, prompting a necessity to increase your level of maturity. When theory, practice and wisdom are equally applied, the output of your work will be clean, clear and above personal gratification. Also, always be large hearted and keep forgiving every day. The more you forgive, the cleaner your conscience becomes.

When I was 11, a majority of family members and friends thought I would become a monk!

When I was 18, people thought I would run away from IIT, as I didn't know English!

When I was 25, given my life style and habits, most of my friends believed I will not reach 50!

I broke all these myths, just by surrendering myself to my work and duties.

A heartfelt
'Thank you'

I am ever so grateful to my parents for having given me education and 'sanskars'. They instilled values that were not just preached, but practiced.

I am also grateful to my sister, brother and a host of my cousins. Each one has a special place in my life.

I am rich with a huge friend circle, right from my childhood. Each one has given me something virtuous, and each in some way or the other has held my hand and supported me when the days seemed bleak. Many of my friends took more interest in my studies compared to their own. I am lucky to have friends like them. My best relationships till date remain the ones that developed by quirk of fate during school and college days.

It has been such a wonderful journey of learning with my colleagues, both past and current, my board members, my bosses, stock brokers, my media friends. I have enjoyed their faith and confidence, trust and unconditional support.

I am grateful to people from the industries like Banking, Mutual funds, NBFCs. Also the Government Officials, Regulators, Musicians, Cricketers, Movie Stars, Investors, Politicians, Doctors, Lawyers, Company Secretaries, Chartered Accountants, and Students.

Life has been like a breeze with huge turbulences between calm phases. Not a moment of boredom. It is amazing that some of my co workers have worked with me for over 25 years and continue to do so. They have tolerated me all along and I hope they will continue to do so.

From a remote suburb of a small town to settling in Mumbai, it has been a journey of over 35 years. Mumbai accepted me and gave me sustenance. Thank you Mumbai

ASHISH CHAUHAN

Ashish Chauhan – Profile

1. Board Member of 'BSE Institute Limited', 'BSE Sammaan Limited', and 'Marketplace Technologies Private Limited'.

2. Member of the Board of Directors - IIM Raipur.

3. Member of the Board of Directors – 'National Institute of Financial Management', Faridabad, appointed by the Government of India.

4. Member of several SEBI committees - Primary Market Advisory Committee, Secondary Market Advisory Committee, Technical Advisory Committee (TAC) on Money, Foreign Exchange and Government Securities Markets of RBI.

5. Member of the National Executive Committee and the Capital Markets Committee of FICCI as well as FICCI's Inclusive Governance Council.

6.	Member of Advisory Committee IBBI – Corporate Insolvency and Liquidation

7.	Served as the Chairman of South Asian Federation of Exchanges (SAFE) from June 2018 to June 2019, a forum of 28-member entities from the SAARC region and neighbouring countries.

8.	Member of the Managing Committee of the Indian Merchants Chamber

9.	Member of the Advisory Committee of the proposed 'Mumbai University School of Economics and Public Policy'.

10.	Member of the Advisory Board of 'Lend a Hand India' – a NGO working in implementing vocational skill development programs for rural and urban youth.

11.	Member of the 'International Leadership Council of Ryerson Futures', an accelerator program that selects and assembles top technology-based startups globally.

12.	Member of the 'UK-India Financial Partnership' and member 'UK-India CEO Council' constituted by the respective Governments.

13.	 Distinguished visiting professor at the Ryerson University in Toronto. Canada

14.	Honorary Professor at the Nottingham University Business School, UK.

15.	Served on the Membership Review Committee of the 'World Federation of Exchanges'.

16.   Served on 'Central Board of Direct Taxes (CBDT)' -
      PNG on Information Technology.

17.   Director – 'Institute of Insolvency Professionals'.

18.   Advisor to the Technical Evaluation Committee -
      Department of Posts for Postal Bank.

19.   Served on several Government and Regulatory
      Committees on 'pro-bono' basis.

20.   Serves on various CII committees – 'National
      Committee on Capital Markets', 'Economic Growth
      and Investments Council', and 'National Council on
      Financial Sector Development' of CII.

21.   Served as the Founder & Chairman of the 'CIO Klub
      of India', with more than 750 Chief Information
      Officers (CIOs) as its members, till 2012.

22.   Recognized among the top 50 Chief Information
      Officers (CIO) by several magazines and institutions
      between 2005 and 2009, including CIO Magazine
      US, Information Week, US etc.

23.   Ranked amongst the 60 most influential Gujarati's
      in the World, for last 2 consecutive years by
      'Chitralekha', the largest selling Gujarati magazine

24.   Advisor – 'Dalit Indian Chamber of Commerce'
      (DICCI).

25.   Ex-Chairman- Board of Governors NIT, Manipur

26.   Ex - member of the Board of Governors of 'Indian
      Institute of Information Technology, Design &
      Manufacturing (IIIT)', Jabalpur

27.   Ex -member of the 'Industry and Business Interface Cell', Banaras Hindu University.

28.   Teaches Finance, Information Technology and several other subjects at Universities in India and abroad.

29.   Speaker at important International and Indian industry events, on various topics.

30.   Actively contributes articles on Information Technology, Market Microstructure, Financial sector Policies, Automation of Markets, Creation of Indices etc. - Books, Newspapers, Magazines and Journals.

Ashish Chauhan – Awards

1. Girnar 'Man of the Year 2019' (Business Category) - Bruhad Mumbai Gujarati Samaj

2. 'Digital Icon of India Inc., 2019' – Hewlett Packard

3. 'Distinguished Fellow, 2017'- Institute of Directors, New Delhi

4. 'Distinguished Alumnus Award, 2016' - IIM Calcutta

5. 'Global Financial Services CEO of the Year, 2016' – Burj CEO Awards, Washington D.C

6. 'CEO of the Year' - Diamond Sabre Awards 2015, Hong Kong

7. 'Indian Business Leader of the Year' - PwC, Horasis Interlaken/Switzerland 2015

8. 'RH Patil Award for Excellence in Financial Services' - June 2015

9.   'Distinguished Alumnus Award' - Indian Institute of Technology, Bombay, 2014

10.   'Best CEO in the Financial Markets in the Asia Pacific' - the Asian Banker, 2014.

11.   'Special contribution in Commodities and Capital Market, 2013' - Zee Business Awards

12.   'Top 50 CIO's' - Information Week US, 2009

13.   'Best IT implementation of India'- PC Quest Magazine India - 2005, 2006, 2007 and 2008

14.   'IT User Award', Manufacturing Sector 2008- NASSCOM, CNBC TV 18.

15.   'Indian Most Admired Knowledge Enterprise (MAKE) Award' 2008 - KNOW Network.

16.   'Excellence in Information Integrity (EII) Award', for profit category, Information Integrity Coalition (IIC) US, Bronze Winner 2008.

17.   'The World Is Open Award'- Red Hat, March 2008

18.   'CIO 100 Award'- Jaipur India, 2008

19.   'CIO Excellence Award' - Chemical Week, Florida, US, 2007

20.   'CIO Hall of Fame Award' - CTO Forum Istanbul, Turkey, 2007

21.   'Skoch Challenger CIO of the Year Award'- February 2007

22.   'CIO of the Year, IT-People'- Mumbai, January 2007

23. 'Technology Senate Intelligent Enterprise Award'-
    Express Computers, India, 2006

24. 'Gold CIO of the Year 2006' and 'Silver CIO of the Year
    2005' Award   - CIOL, with Data Quest Magazine,
    India

25. 'CIO-100 Award' - CIO Magazine, California, US,
    2005

Ashish Chauhan

Ashish Chauhan's family hails from a small hamlet, near Ahmedabad, in Gujarat. Education was of prime importance in his family, both his parents being well educated. But young Ashish was at ease with his studies, never under stress to outperform his peers.

On such a carefree and simple substratum, his higher education and then his professional endeavours, built an edifice of remarkable achievements.

As soon as he secured his first job, it seemed fated that the toughest challenges were just waiting for him! Fearless by nature, each challenge not only gave him an adrenaline rush but also helped him develop many skills, in his quest to find solutions. 'Speed' became his forte and 'Foresight', his fortitude.

Technology was the 'Strategic' tool that he used in many brilliant ways. He encouraged his teams to drive existing or new technologies in different areas to help speed up operations and give faster results.

As the book unfolds, chapter by chapter, we travel along with him on an interesting journey of discipline, hard work, a positive attitude, fearlessness, a balanced mind and above all, selfless service.

His growth trajectory is an inspirational story of how India allows its youth to dream and also to achieve those dreams, provided they put in single minded efforts and work for their fellow beings.

About the Author - Mayoor Shah

He has been writing since his teen years. His short stories and fashion apparel for children were published in weekly editions of newspapers when he was just 14. He has held several exhibitions of his paintings, the first at the age of 17, inaugurated by Late Smt. Nargis Dutt. Graduate in Politics and Sociology, he is a Distinction holder in the study of the 'Vedantas'.

He has diplomas in Business Management, Hotel Management and Textile Designing. He has a keen interest in jewellery designing and interior decoration. As a music lover he has conceptualised over 20 unique musical events and presented them in over 300 stage shows in India and abroad.

He runs a Production House called REFLECTIONS, which is in its
35th year of operations. Being a Creative director, he writes all the scripts. He has produced over 8000 corporate films and ad films. Apart from 5 daily soaps for National Television, his production house has produced two Marathi Feature films, 'DEVKI' and 'VITHAL VITHAL' and won over 50 awards. He has been a Jury of selection of Indian Panorama in the International Film Festivals. He lectures on Communication Skills, Creative Writing etc. at various Management Institutes.

Price : ₹500

www.ingramcontent.com/pod-product-compliance
Lightning Source LLC
Chambersburg PA
CBHW061518120726
48001CB00004B/1353